Celebrating your year

1966

a very special year for

A message from the author:

Welcome to the year 1966.

I trust you will enjoy this fascinating romp down memory lane.

And when you have reached the end of the book, please join me in the battle against AI generated copy-cat books and fake reviews.

Details are near the back of the book.

Best regards,
Bernard Bradforsand-Tyler.

Contents

1966 Family Life in the USA 9
Life in the United Kingdom 13
Our Love Affair with Cars 19
Television's Race to Color 25
Most Popular TV Shows of 1966 26
The Cold War–Nuclear Arms Race 30
The Cold War–Space Race 31
The Cold War–Battlefield Vietnam 34
Anti-Vietnam Protests 35
    Protests and Riots 36
    Disaster at Aberfan 40
    Assassination in South Africa 41
    1966 in Cinema and Film 44
Espionage Films of 1966 46
Top Grossing Films of the Year 47
Musical Memories 50
Wes Wilson's Psychedelic Concert Posters .. 53
    1966 Billboard Top 30 Songs 54
    Fashion Trends of the 1960s 57
    Science and Medicine 65
VIII British Empire & Commonwealth Games .. 68
Also in Sports 69
Other News from 1966 70
Famous People Born in 1966 72
1966 in Numbers 76
Image Attributions 84

Advertisement

Lady, you'll just love flameless electric cooking
(almost this much)

A flameless electric range is the only way to discover just how clean and easy cooking can be. Walls and cabinets stay like new, curtains keep fresh-looking for months on end and your kitchen stays comfortably cool. Only electric ovens have the exclusive new improvements that make them so easy to keep clean. Pick the right moment to talk to your husband about a new flameless electric range—another electric appliance worth loving.

You live better electrically

Throughout America, this Gold Medallion identifies modern homes in which families find the joy of total electric living with flameless home heating and appliances.

Let's flashback to 1966, a very special year.

Was this the year you were born?

Was this the year you were married?

Whatever the reason, this book is a celebration of your year,

THE YEAR 1966.

Turn the pages to discover a book packed with fun-filled fabulous facts. We look at the people, the places, the politics and the pleasures that made 1966 unique and helped shape the world we know today.

So get your time-travel suit on, and enjoy this trip down memory lane, to rediscover what life was like, back in the year 1966.

Advertisement

So what?

The new Bronica S2 doesn't really offer very much over any other 2¼-square single lens reflex if you leave out the automatic return mirror, the automatic reopen diaphragm, interchangeable film backs, interchangeable Nikkor lenses, and high-speed focal-plane shutter.

By why leave them out when they add so much to operating ease and performance. And it costs you no more to enjoy them. Bronica S2 with 75mm Auto-Nikkor f2.8 lens is $479.50.

If you must leave something out, consider the Bronica C. Costs you $100 less. Substantially the same as the S2, except it doesn't have interchangeable film backs. Has interchangeable film inserts, though, like the S2, which handle 220 as well as 120 roll film.

Let your dealer also show you the Bronica system of lenses and accessories.

BRONICA division of Ehrenreich Photo-Optical Industries, Inc., Garden City, N.Y. 11533

1966 Family Life in the USA

Imagine if time-travel was a reality, and one fine morning you wake up to find yourself flashed back in time, back to the year 1966.

What would life be like for a typical family, in a typical town, somewhere in America?

Young family relaxing at home in 1966.

The 1960s was a decade of change, of shifting social movements, of vibrant and vocal youth, of rebellion and rejection. Yet, what we fondly refer to as "The Sixties", really only began in the middle of the decade.

The first half of the decade more rightly belonged to the Post-War era, also known as the Golden Years, the era of the Baby Boomers (1946-1964).

76.4 million Americans had been born during the Baby Boom years, accounting for 40% of our population. By 1966, the first of the Baby Boomers were making themselves heard. Their views, aspirations and demands would shape America, and the world, for decades to come.

By 1966, we'd grown tired of our post-war traditional conservative family values. Our youth had discovered a new energy, in the exciting movements sweeping the UK. London's Mods and Swinging Sixties encouraged freedom of expression, liberation, and rejection of the constraints of our old-world order. The "British Invasion" conquered the world through music, art, film, and fashion.

America's youth just couldn't get enough of all things British. We had time to indulge in life's pleasures, we had money to spare.

The Rolling Stones in the mid-'60s.

Sean Connery as James Bond.

Beatlemania, fans at Shea Stadium, 15th Aug 1965.

During the '60s, we benefited from America's longest ever period of continuous economic growth, averaging 5% GDP growth annually, peaking at around 6.5% during 1965 and 1966.

We were more likely to be working in offices, rather than tilling the land or working on assembly lines. We had more spending power than ever before. And we enjoyed an excessive consume-and-discard culture, driven by a mature advertising industry which instilled in us the belief that we constantly needed more and more, bigger and better.

But beyond pleasure-filled amusement and leisure time, we were also fighting for a better world. Students rallied against the draft, feminists demanded gender equality, African Americans marched for civil rights, professors held teach-ins, and everywhere, our citizens were standing up against US involvement in the Vietnam War.

June 1966 – The Memphis to Mississippi 21-day *March Against Fear* attracted more than 15,000 marchers.

Average costs in 1966 [1]	
New house	$20,705
New car	$2,650
Refrigerator	$220
Washing Machine	$160
A gallon of gasoline	$0.31

The median family income was $7,400 a year.[2]
Unemployment stood at 3.8%, with GDP growth at 6.6%.[3]

[1] thepeoplehistory.com and mclib.info/reference/local-history-genealogy/historic-prices/.
[2] census.gov/library/publications/1967/demo/p60-052.html.
[3] thebalance.com/unemployment-rate-by-year-3305506.

Advertisement

BIG HOTPOINT SUMMER SALE

NEW! LOW-PRICED! "No-Frost 17" $298*
No-Frost Freezer • No-Frost Refrigerator

3 beautiful ways to save money!

New "No-Frost 17" refrigerator rolls out on wheels for easy cleaning

Big inside—16.6 cu. ft. N.E.M.A. capacity—yet only 32" wide and 65½" tall. Fits kitchens like older 12 footers. You get a 12.7 cu. ft. No-Frost refrigerator section and a 1.38 lb. No-Frost freezer section. There's a separate temperature-control for both refrigerator and freezer. Greatest refrigerator value ever! Model CTF117G. **Low priced $298***

Multi-cycle, 2 speed washer has 16 lb. capacity —all-porcelain finish **Low priced $189***

Washer handles 2 to 16 pound loads. Two speeds, multi-cycle, three wash temperatures and three water levels give you better results with all your laundry. Has all-porcelain finish outside and in. Model LW670.

New Total-Clean range has oven walls you slide out, sponge clean **Low priced $199***

Easy to clean all over! Removable Teflon-coated oven walls—plus oven door, storage drawer and drip pans that slip off for quick cleaning. Model RB540.

*Prices and terms optional with your local Hotpoint dealer, except where fair traded. Prices higher in Hawaii.

Hotpoint
first with the features women want most
Hotpoint—General Electric Co. • Chicago, Illinois 60644

3 beautiful ways to save money!

New "No-Frost 17" refrigerator rolls out on wheels for easy cleaning. Big inside– 16.6 cu. ft. N.E.M.A. capacity–yet only 32" wide and 65$^1/_2$" tall. Fits kitchen like older 12 footers. You get a 12.7 cu. ft. No-Frost refrigerator section and a 1.38lb. No-Frost freezer section. There's a separate temperature-control for both refrigerator and freezer. Greatest refrigerator value ever! Model CTF117G. Low priced $298.

Multi-cycle, 2 speed washer has 16 lb. capacity–all porcelain finish. Washer handles 2 to 16 pound loads. Two speeds, multi-cycle, three wash temperatures and three water levels give you better results with your laundry. Has all-porcelain finish outside and in. Model LW670. Low priced $189.

New Total-Clean range has oven walls you slide out, sponge clean. Easy to clean all over! Removable Teflon-coated oven walls–plus oven door, storage drawer and drip pans that slip off for quick cleaning. Model RB540. Low priced $199.

Life in the United Kingdom

Now just imagine you flashed back to a town in 1966 England or Western Europe.

London's "Swinging Sixties" was now center stage for music, arts, fashion, and all things cultural.

With the ravages of war firmly in the past, the cultural revolution known as the Swinging Sixties quickly became the United Kingdom's greatest export of the decade. Focused on fun-loving hedonism and rejection of traditional conservatism, this was a revolution full of excitement, freedom and hope. Unlike their American counterparts, UK's Baby Boomers were free of conscription and the miseries of war.

Turning heads in the latest fashions on Carnaby Street, London, 1966.

Artists, musicians, writers, designers, filmmakers, photographers, and all types of creatives and intellectuals descended on London. Their radical views brought about a revolution in social and sexual politics.

The Who, 1966.

Musicians led the charge with their own uniquely British sound. Influenced by rock 'n' roll of the '50s, yet infused with innovative new rhythms and sounds, their songs inspired their fans to express individuality and freedom.

The Beatles.

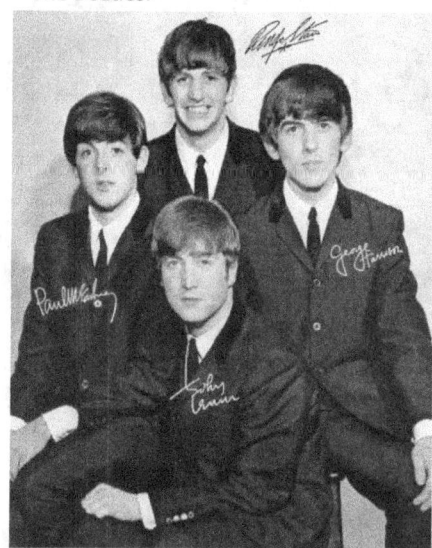

The Rolling Stones, 1966.

Pirate radio stations brought "the London Sound" to the airwaves, pushing bands like The Rolling Stones, The Kinks, The Yardbirds, and The Who, along with early '60s mega-band The Beatles.

In fashion, designer Mary Quant created youthful styles for running, jumping and dancing in. Along with other trend-setting designers, the fashion scene centered around London's Carnaby Street and King's Road in Kensington.

London also introduced us to the first non-aristocratic looking supermodels, who soon became household names. Through magazines worldwide, they guided us on the newest trends in urban style and street wear.

'60s supermodels Jean Shrimpton and Twiggy.

In literature, retired British spy Jean Le Carré penned unstoppable mystery thrillers infused with cold-war espionage. He, along with crowd-pleasing British favorites like Agatha Christie, Alistair MacLean, and Victor Canning, became instant International best sellers.

British film-makers captured the high-spirited fun and sexual freedom of swinging London with experimental, mischievous comedies focused on themes of escape and young, free love.

THE ROYAL TOUCH

For offices, schools or homes, it's the most easy-going, self-reliant, sweet-typing, money-saving, good-looking Royal family of electric, manual and portable typewriters.

Ask the girls: students, top executives' secretaries, professional women. They'll tell you they can always spot a Royal by the touch. The Royal Touch on electrics, manuals and portables is light, responsive, smooth, nimble. Uniquely so.

Behind that Royal Touch are 60 years of engineering and manufacturing experience. And a testing program that's rigid and rigorous. Before any Royal typewriter goes out into the world (whether it's the full-featured office Electress, the ruggedly dependable Empress® Manual or a sturdy Royal portable), every part and every action is tested, checked — then checked again. When you buy a Royal, you can be sure it'll have that light and easy touch... the one-and-only Royal Touch.

ROYAL® McBEE
CORPORATION

The sweet-typing Royal Touch, left to right is on the Empress (sturdiest, most service-free manual) on the Electress (two executives' secretaries prefer it) and the Sahara® Portable (with a glamorous travel case, for girls on the go).

Every year more Royal typewriters are bought in America than any other brand.

The Royal Touch   For offices, schools or homes, it's them most easy-going, self-reliant, sweet-typing, money-saving, good-looking Royal family of electric, manual and portable typewriters.

Ask the girls: students, top executives' secretaries, professional women. They'll tell you that they can always spot a Royal by the touch. The Royal Touch on electrics, manuals and portables is light, responsive, smooth, nimble. Uniquely so.

Behind that Royal Touch are 60 years of engineering and manufacturing experience. And a testing program that's rigid and rigorous. Before any Royal typewriter goes out into the world (whether it's the full-featured office Electress, the ruggedly dependable Empress Manual or a sturdy Royal portable), every part and every action is tested, checked—then checked again. When you buy a Royal, you can be sure it'll have that light and easy touch... the one-and-only Royal Touch.

Every year more Royal typewriters are bought in America than any other brand.

Swinging London was largely seen as a middle-class consumer-driven diversion, centered around the fashionable West End. Elsewhere, counter sub-cultures existed, such as the Mods and the Rockers. The groups were easily identified by their outfits and choice of vehicles, the Rockers on their motorbikes wore leather jackets, while the Mods on their mirror-decked scooters preferred Italian-cut suits.

In 1964 violent clashes between the Rockers and Mods erupted, leaving both groups branded as trouble-makers.

Throughout the decade, British families gained greater purchasing power and disposable incomes. Stable economic growth led to rising living standards with excess cash for leisure and amusements.

Home ownership rose markedly as a 20-year post-war construction boom provided much needed affordable housing stock. A "job for life" was a reality, and job security made home ownership widely attainable.

Education for girls, and the growth of feminism, saw more young women entering the workforce. Although equality was still a long way off, it was now possible to be female, single, living away from home, and independent.

Advertisement

HERE RIDE AMERICA'S MOST LOYAL OWNERS. More Cadillac drivers stay with Cadillac than with any other car built in the land. Now, for 1966, Cadillac provides more driving pleasure than ever before. There is new interior luxury surpassing any Cadillac of the past. New variable ratio power steering and many improvements in suspension, chassis, handling and acoustics make the 1966 Cadillac even quieter and easier to drive. Try it soon and see for yourself! *New elegance, new excellence, new excitement!*

Cadillac Motor Car Division • General Motors Corporation

Here ride America's most loyal owners.

More Cadillac drivers stay with Cadillac than with any other car built in the land. Now, for 1966, Cadillac provides more driving pleasure than ever before. There is new interior luxury surpassing any Cadillac of the past. New variable ration power steering and many improvements in suspension, chassis, handling and acoustics make the 1966 Cadillac even quieter and easier to drive. Try it soon and see for yourself! *New elegance, new excellence, new excitement!*

Cadillac 1966

Our Love Affair with Cars

Our love affair with cars began way back in the early '50s, and by 1966 we were irreversibly addicted to our vehicles. Vehicle numbers continued to rise year-on-year as the cost of a standard family car became increasingly more affordable. Although car costs had risen markedly, so too had real wages.

Increased car ownership and the creation of the National Highway System gave Americans a new sense of freedom. Office commuters could live further out from the crowded and decaying city centers, and commute quickly and comfortably to work.

Rush hour traffic, New York in the 1960s.

Rural areas were no longer isolated, benefiting from access to food, medical and other supplies. The suburbanization of America, which had begun in the early '50s, now saw 40% of the population living in the suburbs. The car was no longer a luxury, it was a necessity.

Northland Mall carpark in the mid-'60s, Columbus, Ohio.

Catering to the suburban lifestyle, fully enclosed, air-conditioned shopping malls sprang up country-wide during the 1960s. A typical mall design saw one or two anchor stores surrounded by hundreds of smaller specialty shops, sitting within a vast expanse of carparks.

Advertisement

Does Pontiac have a one-track mind? Yes. Wide-Track.

Our designers are in a rut. They've been producing winners with such amazing consistency that it hardly seems fair to other car makers. Witness the '67 Bonneville Wide-Track above. Its incredibly sleek lines are even more so this year, due to the fact that our engineers hid the windshield wipers under the cowl. Under the hood they planted a new 400 cubic inch V-8 that'll make dull driving a dim memory. And they've added new safety features like retracting front seat belts, a four-way hazard warning flasher and General Motors' energy absorbing steering column. In fact, if our engineers keep coming up with winners like this, someone may insist they take a year off and give the competition a chance to catch up. That'll be the day.

Pontiac 67/Ride the Wide-Track Winning Streak

Does Pontiac have a one-track mind? Yes. Wide-Track.

Our designers are in a rut. They've been producing winners with such amazing consistency that it hardly seems fair to other car makers. Witness the '67 Bonnevill Wide-Track above. Its incredibly sleek lines are even more so this year, due to the fact that our engineers hid the windshield wipers under the cowl. Under the hood they planted a new 400 cubic inch V-8 that'll make dull driving a dim memory. And they've added new safety features like retracting front seat belts, a four-way hazard warning flasher and General Motors' energy absorbing steering column. In fact, if our engineers keep coming up with winners like this, someone may insist they take a year off and give the competition a chance to catch up. That'll be the day.

Pontiac 67/Ride the Wide-Track Winning Streak

Detroit was America's car manufacturing powerhouse, where "the Big Three" (Ford, General Motors and Chrysler) produced 90% of cars sold in the country. Using technological innovation, with significant financial and marketing strength, the Big Three successfully bought out or edged out all smaller competitors throughout the 1950s and 1960s.

1966 Wide-Track Pontiac.

Big cars ruled the roads during the "Golden Age of Muscle Cars" (1964-1970). These high-performance coupes usually came with large, powerful V-8 engines and rear wheel drive. Also known as "super cars" they were designed with drag-racing engine capability to satisfy our desire for power above all else.

By 1966 there were 77.7 million vehicles on US roads. Car sales were at all-time highs, as were motor vehicle fatalities.

50,894 car-related deaths were recorded during the year, the result of dangerous driving and unsafe vehicles.[1]

1966 Dodge Monaco by Chrysler.

On 10th February 1966, author and activist Ralph Nader testified before Congress on the dangers inherent in the automobile industry. His bestselling book, *Unsafe at Any Speed: The Designed-In Dangers of the American Automobile,* caused sufficient public outcry to push legislators into action. Federal safety standards for new cars would be in place before the year's end.

[1] en.wikipedia.org/wiki/Motor_vehicle_fatality_rate_in_U.S._by_year.

Five car-producing countries dominated the industry in the first half of the decade: England, France, Germany and Italy, with America in top spot. However, Japan stormed into this elite group with a swift and dramatic expansion of its automobile industry. By 1966, Japan was placed third for total number of vehicles produced. Within one year it would pass Germany to be in second place, behind only America.

Japanese domestic demand had grown rapidly in the early '60s through sales of ultra-compact and affordable *kei cars*. Mass production of midsize family cars, more suited to international export, soon followed.

1966 Mazda 800.

Japanese cars were safer to drive, reliable, affordable, compact, efficient and popular, quickly making Toyota, Nissan, Mitsubishi, Mazda and Honda the export market leaders. By 1966, the Japanese automobile industry was on its way to world domination.

1966 Datsun 1600.

1966 Honda S600.

Advertisement

**You're probably in the Chrysler class right now
—and don't even know it.**

Lots of people start out in the same predicament.

They go shop the most popular smaller cars and think, "If these cost this much, imagine how much the big ones are!"

The fact is, they're in Chrysler territory and don't realize it.

The Chrysler above (in our new Bronze color) is priced just a few dollars a month more than the cars they've been looking at, comparably equipped.

That means with a big V-8, automatic transmission, power brakes and steering, radio, heater and whitewalls.

Chrysler also gives you all the new standard safety features—seat belts, padded dash, back-up lights and so on—plus some exclusives of our own.

Now that you know how much more your money can buy, see your Chrysler dealer and move up... move now.

CHRYSLER DIVISION — CHRYSLER MOTORS CORPORATION

Advertisement

Get the big picture!
New Admiral 21" Portable with life-size rectangular screen... from $159.95!

Admiral MARK OF QUALITY THROUGHOUT THE WORLD

Get the big picture!

New Admiral 21" Portable with life-size rectangular screen... from $159.95!
It's almost all picture, this new 21" Portable TV, originated and developed by Admiral! 40 square inches more picture than ordinary 19" TV... on a flat-faced, movie-square screen... in the same size cabinet as most 19's!

Admiral quality precision-engineering hugs the components to the tube, makes it secure to take the jolts and jars a portable gets. Out-front speaker for richer sound, new slide-rule dial for UHF turning. Telescopic dipole antenna, all 82 UHF/VHF channels. See this slim new Admiral 21" Portable TV... *there's nothing finer at any price.*

Admiral. Mark of quality throughout the world.

Television's Race to Color

Those of us old enough will remember when black and white television was the norm. We neither questioned it nor demanded anything different. However, the 1965-1966 season was color TV's breakthrough year, when the three major networks sparked a race-to-color war.

By the end of the season, all three networks aired their entire primetime programs in color. There remained one minor problem however—most households did not own a color TV set.

By 1966, 93% of American households owned a television set (84% in the UK)[1], of which only 10% were color. By 1971 that figure would jump to nearly 50%.[2]

Family TV time in the mid-'60s.

Elsewhere in the world, access to color TV lagged behind the USA. Canada first received color emissions in 1966, with the UK following in 1967. Australia would wait till 1975 for their first color TV broadcasts.

In many countries, television networks were government owned or subsidized, allowing for more focus on serious documentaries and news, without the constant concern of generating advertising revenue.

[1] https://americancentury.omeka.wlu.edu/items/show/136.
[2] tvobscurities.com/articles/color60s/.

Most Popular TV Shows of 1966

1	Bonanza	=	The Virginian
2	The Red Skelton Hour	=	The Lawrence Welk Show
3	The Andy Griffith Show	=	The Ed Sullivan Show
4	The Lucy Show	14	The Dean Martin Show
5	The Jackie Gleason Show	=	Family Affair
6	Green Acres	16	The Smothers Brothers Comedy Hour
7	Daktari	17	Friday Night Movies
=	Bewitched	=	Hogan's Heroes
=	The Beverly Hillbillies	19	Walt Disney's Wonderful World of Color
10	Gomer Pyle, U.S.M.C.	20	Saturday Night at the Movies

*From the Nielsen Media Research 1966-'67 season of top-rated primetime TV series in the USA.

Musical variety shows remained ever popular in 1966, with westerns and dramas added to the mix. But sitcoms continued to pull the highest ratings, with six of the top ten programs of 1966 being situation comedies.

Lucille Ball and Vivian Vance in *The Lucy Show* (CBS. 1962-1968).

Eddie Albert and Eva Gabor in *Green Acres* (CBS. 1965-1971).

Elizabeth Montgomery, Dick York and Agnes Moorehead in *Bewitched* (ABC. 1964-1972).

The Lucy Show was Lucille Ball's follow-up to the hugely successful *I Love Lucy*. Ball would win Emmy Awards for the 1967 and 1968 seasons.

The sitcom fantasy *Bewitched* aired for eight seasons in the '60s and continues to air today as international reruns.

Leonard Nimoy and William Shatner in the original *Star Trek* series (NBC. 1966-1969).

Steven Hill and Martin Landau in *Mission Impossible* (CBS. 1966-1973).

The television networks were quick to turn out new programs to keep us tuning in. Here are just a few of the new programs that aired for the first time in 1966: *Daktari, Family Affair,* and *Tarzan*. Other notables include *Mission Impossible, The Marvel Super Heroes, The Rat Patrol, Till Death Us Do Part (BBC1, UK)*, and the original series of *Star Trek*.

Marshall Thompson with Judy in *Daktari* (CBS. 1966-1969).

Kathy Garver, Anissa Jones, Johnny Whitaker, Brian Keith & Sebastian Cabot in *Family Affair* (CBS. 1966-1971).

Advertisement

Only Swanson gives you an extra "home style" touch like this Pepperidge Farm Recipe blueberry muffin!

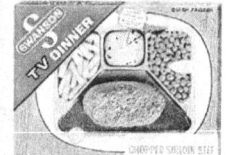

Now Swanson brightens up this Chopped Sirloin Dinner with a fluffy blueberry muffin.

(Almost makes a party out of "Swanson Night")

Juicy, tender all-sirloin chopped steak with gravy. Crisp french fries. Peas in butter sauce for extra flavor. And for an extra festive touch— a warm blueberry muffin. There must be someone's birthday or anniversary or something you could celebrate tonight!

Declare a "Swanson Night"—you can TRUST SWANSON

Only Swanson gives you an extra "home style" touch like this Pepperidge Farm Recipe blueberry muffin!

Now Swanson brightens up this Chopped Sirloin Dinner with a fluffy blueberry muffin. (Almost makes a party out of "Swanson Night")

Juicy, tender all-sirloin chopped steak with gravy. Crisp French fries. Peas in butter sauce for extra flavor. And for an extra festive touch–a warm blueberry muffin. There must be someone's birthday or anniversary or something you could celebrate tonight!

Declare a "Swanson Night"–you can Trust Swanson

Advertisement

We've never limited our thinking to automobiles.

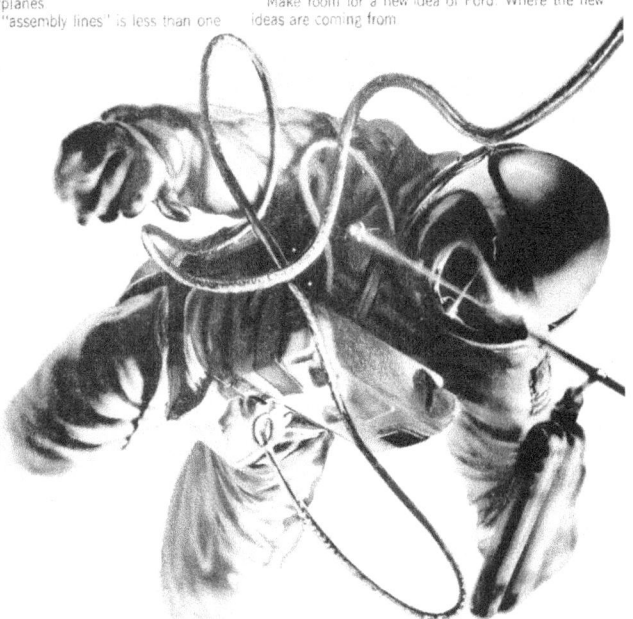

We've never limited our thinking to automobiles.

Sure, we're the people who build cars–from Mustangs to Lincoln Continentals. And the same people who come up with some of the newest ideas in cars–like 2-way tailgates, Stereo-Sonic Tape Systems. But that doesn't mean when we build a Philco refrigerator, we put a dashboard in it.

We've never limited our thinking to automobiles.

A far back as 40 years ago we were making trucks, tractor plows and airplanes. Today one of our "assembly lines" is less than one inch long. Making Philco microcircuits for the Apollo Block II guidance computer. Others are producing air conditioners... color TV... communication systems... Autolite spark plugs. We designed NASA's huge Mission Control Center in Houston. (Try putting that in your garage.)

The point is–next time you see our familiar Ford trademark, please make room in your mind for more than cars. Make room for a new idea of Ford. Where the new ideas are coming from.

The Cold War-Nuclear Arms Race

Cold War tensions between the two former allies–the USSR and the USA–had been building during the 1950s and dominated our lives throughout the 1960s.

Starting in the USA as policies for communist containment, the distrust and misunderstanding between the two sides quickly escalated from political squabbling, to a military nuclear arms race. Trillions of dollars in military spending saw both sides stockpile their nuclear arsenals, strategically positioning and pointing their missiles closer and closer to each other.

During the 1960s, America's global nuclear weapon stockpiles increased rapidly, peaking in 1967. By 1966, the USA held 31,175 nuclear weapons, against the Soviet's 7,090 weapons. Joining the superpowers in this elite group were–the UK (380 weapons), France (36 weapons), and China (20 weapons).[1]

The 1960s also saw a rapid escalation in nuclear weapons testing. These tests served to understand the effectiveness and capacity of each bomb type. They also acted as a deterrent to enemy nations.

In 1966, the USA carried out 48 nuclear tests, mostly at the Nevada Proving Grounds, while USSR tested 18 nuclear bombs. Although most of the test sites were largely uninhabited by humans, some of them were densely populated. The effects of radioactive fallout plagued local populations for years afterwards.

19th Dec– The UN approved a treaty to ban nuclear weapons in outer space.

[1] tandfonline.com/doi/pdf/10.2968/066004008.

Bomb test at the Nevada Proving Grounds, circa 1960s.

The Cold War–Space Race

Throughout the 1960s, the Cold War dominated our lives on the ground and in the skies. Cold War tensions affected everything from our politics and education, to our interests in fashion and popular culture. During this time, the USSR achieved many firsts, putting them at a military, technological and intellectual advantage.

Sputnik 1 was the world's first artificial earth satellite, launched into orbit in 1957. Yuri Gagarin became the first human to orbit the earth in 1961, and Valentina Tereshkova became the first woman in space in 1963. On 18th March 1965, Alexei Leonov became the first human to walk in space.

The USSR continued to take the lead with longer space flights and space walks, and other complex activities. On 3rd February 1966, after 12 attempts, Luna 9 became the first spacecraft to successfully land on the moon.

Yuri Gagarin, first man in space.

Valentina Tereshkova, first woman in space.

Alexei Leonov, first person to walk in space.

The US responded by increasing spending on education and defense in a bid to catch up with the Soviets. NASA had been established in 1958, and in 1961, US President John F. Kennedy declared that America would land a man on the moon. The space race was on.

Advertisement

HAVEN'T TRIED SMIRNOFF? WHERE IN THE WORLD HAVE YOU BEEN?

You've really been out of touch if you haven't explored Smirnoff with orange juice, with tomato juice, with 7-Up® (in the new Smirnoff Mule). Or discovered that Smirnoff makes the dryest Martinis, the smoothest drink on-the-rocks. Only Smirnoff, filtered through 14,000 pounds of activated charcoal, makes so many drinks so well. Why wait? Let the next Smirnoff launching be *yours!*

Get acquainted offer: Try the delicious drinks you've been missing with this new half quart sampler bottle. Now available in most states.

Haven't tried Smirnoff? Where in the world have you been?

You've really been out of touch if you haven't explored Smirnoff with orange juice, with tomato juice, with 7-Up (in the new Smirnoff Mule). Or discovered that Smirnoff makes the driest Martinis, the smoothest drink on-the-rocks. Only Smirnoff, filtered through 14,000 pounds of activated charcoal, makes so many drinks so well. Why wait? Let the next Smirnoff launching be *yours!*

Always ask for Smirnoff vodka. It leaves you breathless.

During 1965 and 1966, NASA conducted ten Project Gemini missions. The missions sought to test the endurance of the space crews and space equipment. Complex maneuvers such as space walks, rendezvous and docking, were designed to train the astronauts to survive in space for longer and longer periods.

The Gemini Program proved humans could fly the duration needed to reach the moon and back and perform any required tasks outside of the spacecraft.

NASA was ready for the next phase— the Apollo moon missions. Pilots Neil Armstrong, Edwin "Buzz" Aldrin and James A. Lovell of later Apollo missions, also took part in the Project Gemini missions. The USA would achieve its goal, winning the space race in 1969, when Apollo 11 brought Armstrong and Aldrin to the moon for their historic lunar walk, lasting $2^1/_4$ hours.

Astronaut Ed White outside Gemini 4, the first American to "spacewalk", 3rd June '65.

Right – Commander Neil Armstrong (front) and pilot David R. Scott prepare to board the Gemini-Titan VIII, 16th March 1966.

Below – Buzz Aldrin walks on the moon. Photo by Neil Armstrong, 20th July 1969.

The Cold War–Battlefield Vietnam

Fearful that a "domino effect" would see an uncontained spread of communism across the world, the US committed to supporting South Vietnam, financially and militarily, during its 30-year-long bloody civil war against North Vietnam (the Viet Cong). In support of the enemy, communist China and USSR were jointly aiding the Viet Cong's invasion southward. Vietnam had become a Cold War battlefield.

America's involvement in the Vietnam War (known in Vietnam as the American War) drastically intensified during the mid-'60s, when President Johnson ordered hundreds of thousands of US combat forces to be sent to Vietnam.

By the end of 1966, 385,000 American troops were deployed in Vietnam. Heavy bombing raids had been carried out against the Viet Cong around Saigon, in North Vietnam, along the Cambodian border, and through secret CIA sponsored operations in Laos.

Despite heavy losses on both sides (6,000 US troops against 61,000 Viet Cong),[1] the Viet Cong grew in numbers and were ever elusive in the jungle.

As the war dragged on, US soldiers were beset with rising casualties, physical and psychological stress, and increasing distrust of their own government. Forced to fight a war they didn't believe in, morale among the draftees was low. Drug usage became rampant. It is estimated up to 50% of US soldiers experimented with marijuana, opium and heroin, cheaply available on the streets of Saigon. US military hospitals would later report drug abuse victims far outnumbered actual war casualties.

[1] pbs.org/battlefieldvietnam/timeline/index1.html#.

Anti-Vietnam Protests

Although most Americans supported the country's involvement in the Vietnam, a vocal group of intellectuals, students and artists had begun speaking out against what they believed was an immoral war.

By 1966, anti-war protests had spilled from the campuses to the city streets. The protestors argued that the foreign powers had secret imperialistic intentions in Asia and shouldn't be involved in this civil war. Large-scale protests were being held across the US, in London, Paris, Rome, and Sydney, growing into a global Peace Movement.

The US Airforce regularly attacked Viet Cong hideouts with toxic chemical weapons, attempting to clear the jungle's dense foliage. 20 million gallons of herbicides, including Agent Orange, were sprayed over Vietnam, Laos and Cambodia during the decade.[1] Cancers, birth defects and other serious health issues resulted.

Media coverage helped expose the brutality of the war and the true number of casualties. The Peace Movement was boosted by those opposed to the draft, which drew unfairly from the minorities and the less wealthy. African Americans, religious leaders, veterans, soldiers and parents also joined.

[1] history.com/topics/vietnam-war/agent-orange-1.

Protests and Riots

The anti-Vietnam War protests were just one of many social change movements to rock affluent Western nations in 1966. The women's movement, the students movement, the gay rights movement and the environmental movement all made their mark during the year, changing our view of the world, and ultimately government policy.

In the USA, the Civil Rights protests were among the most visible of all the social change movements. Demonstrations by African Americans and their supporters had been gaining momentum for the preceding ten years, and would reach a tipping point the following year, in what would become known as the 1967 "long, hot summer" of riots.

The Hough riots, 18th-23rd July, Cleveland, Ohio. – For four nights, bands of youths roamed the streets, clashing with police over the systemic racial injustice endured by the predominately black residents of Hough. Sparked by a minor racial dispute, widespread looting, arson and destruction followed.

Marquette Park Rallies, 31st Jul-5th Aug, Chicago, Illinois. – Aiming to address racial discrimination in housing, several hundreds marched to Marquette Park on 31st July, and again, led by Martin Luther King Jr. on 5th August. They were attacked on both occasions by "hostile and hate-filled" white counter-protestors waving swastikas and confederate flags.

Division Street riots, 12th-14th June, Chicago, Illinois. – An altercation between police and a young Puerto Rican attracted a small crowd of onlookers, which soon grew to over 4,000 as more police arrived. Over 3 days of violence, fifty buildings were looted and destroyed. The riots inspired the Puerto Rican community to form action groups to fight against oppression and discrimination.

Compton's Cafeteria riot, August, San Francisco, California. – Police were regularly called to remove, harass, or arrest the drag queens and transgender customers of Compton's for the crime of "female impersonation". A riot began when one customer resisted arrest, throwing a cup of coffee in a policeman's face.

Chaos erupted as police were attacked with handbags, stilettos, chairs and tableware. Fighting spilled into the streets, continuing the next night. This event marked the beginning of LGBT activism.

Sunset Strip curfew riots, West Hollywood, California. – The "hippie riots" centered around Sunset Strip saw year-long clashes between police and the young followers of hippie or rock 'n' roll countercultures. Strict 10pm curfew and loitering laws were considered an infringement of civil rights. On 12th Nov, a rally outside Pandora's Box club attracted 1,000 protestors, including Hollywood celebrities. Protests continued for months. It was the start of the generational culture wars.

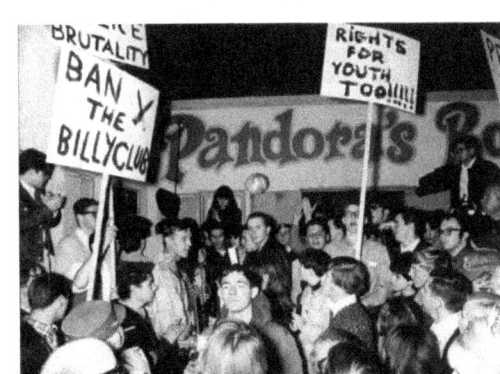

Advertisement

Want to read a good book?

We don't just mean good for you. We mean good. It's our unorthodox notion that an encyclopedia should be a book full of absorbing reading. Not just a grab-bag full of look-up-able facts. Of course the facts must be there. Complete and accurate. But, as every student knows, a poor teacher can make facts muddy and boring. A great teacher can make the same facts come to life. So, when we go scouting for people to write for the Americana, we hunt for experts who know more than their facts. We don't want experts who need experts to understand them. We want writer-experts—who know how to make a page teach.

Open any one of our thirty volumes. We think you'll see the difference at once. Say you've turned to the entry on Space Research. Here's the first sentence you'll read: "Ninety-three million miles from the luminous sphere called the sun, the planet earth moves through empty space, wrapped in a thin cloud-flecked veil called the atmosphere."

And now you're off. Moving as easily through the facts of space as you would through a science-fiction story. Which isn't really surprising. The author is Dr. Willy Ley. He's been in space engineering since its beginning. But he's also a writer with several science-fiction credits to his name. Then there's our biography of Poe. It reads like a novel. It ought to. It was written by the celebrated author-critic, Joseph Wood Krutch. You probably know the two writer-experts we've just talked about. We have many other contributors whose names you'd know as well. Famous scientist-writers, historian-writers, artist-writers. Yet we sometimes bypass the most famous man—the best known man in his field—for a less publicized expert who writes more clearly and vividly. We feel it's the quality of the writing that makes the Encyclopedia Americana such a good book. Like any other good book, it's hard to put down.

Advertisement

Why is Western Electric so proud of this old sewing machine when we're really in the telephone business?

Because it still works. A Connecticut housewife still relies on it. When Western Electric sold it to her mother in 1918, we backed it with a solid five-year guarantee which, of course, expired unnoticed. Even in those days, reliability was a matter of prime importance to Western Electric.

We haven't sold electrical appliances like sewing machines for more than a generation because we concentrate on our main business—providing Bell telephones and other equipment that makes them serve the public so well. And our standards for reliability are even higher today.

Take your Bell telephone for example. How long has it been since it needed repair—if ever? Even though our experience in communications goes back ninety-six years, our job as manufacturing and supply unit of the Bell System gets tougher each year. Unlike a sewing machine, your Bell telephone is interconnected to millions of others. This requires a nationwide network of literally billions of parts. Every part of it—down to the tiniest component—must be made to work dependably—each with each as one unified system.

So you see why we're so strict about quality. It's one of the ways we help your Bell telephone company bring you efficient, dependable communications services at low cost.

Disaster at Aberfan

21st October 1966

116 children perished, along with 28 adults, when 140,000 cubic yards (110,000 m³) of coal waste slid into the Pantglas Junior School and adjoining houses at 9am on 21st October 1966. The landslide of the colliery spoil tip followed weeks of heavy rain, which had turned the coal waste into slurry.

Built on the side of a mountain above the Welsh mining village of Aberfan, UK, the tip was one of seven surrounding the village. Three had been constructed on the mountain side above underground streams. It was not the first time heavy rains had made the tips unstable, and resident's concerns had been raised following minor landslides in earlier years.

Aerial footage of Aberfan taken after the landslide.

Local residents rushed to the disaster site in the immediate aftermath and began frantically digging through the rubble with their bare hands. Before long, teams of coal miners arrived, working in organized groups to clear the debris and lift out any survivors, before locating the deceased. It would be one week before all the bodies were located.

After an official inquiry found that the colliery waste tip should never have been built above an underground stream, the National Coal Board received full blame for the disaster. However, the organization was not fined, and none of its employees were ever prosecuted.

Assassination in South Africa

6th September 1966

South African Prime Minister Hendrik Verwoerd was stabbed to death during a parliamentary meeting in the House of Assembly. His assassin, Demetrio Tsafendas, inflicted four stab wounds to the neck and chest before being subdued by other members of the Assembly.

Regarded as the architect of Apartheid (apartness), Verwoerd solidified systemic racial segregation during his time as Minister of Native Affairs (1950–58) and as Prime Minister (1958–66). He actively shaped Apartheid's white supremacist laws, reinforcing white dominance over the majority non-white population.

Verwoerd's policies restricted land ownership and occupation to specific racial groups within specific areas, allowing for forcible, and often violent, removal of non-whites from white designated areas. Restricted access to voting and education ensured the non-white citizens remained oppressed.

Tsafendas had a long history of anti-apartheid activism, and he saw Verwoerd's death as a necessary first step to bring about positive change in the country. However, his political beliefs and activism were never mentioned during trial. He pleaded insanity to avoid execution.

Tsafendas was found not guilty of murder by reason of insanity. He would spend 28 years in prison, and the remaining five years of his life in a psychiatric institution. It is now widely accepted that Tsafendas was not at all insane, he was a courageous anti-apartheid activist, seen by many as a revolutionary hero.[1]

---

[1] Dousemetzis, Harris; Loughran, Gerry (2018). *The Man Who Killed Apartheid: The Life of Dimitri Tsafendas*. Johannesburg: Jacana Media. ISBN 9781431427543.

Advertisement

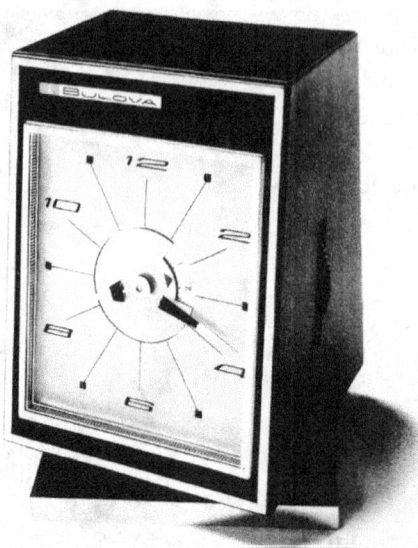

This Bulova cordless electric clock gives you the news.

Because it's also a cordless radio.
The world's only completely cordless radio-clock.

A tiny transistorized radio. Put back to back to a precision-jeweled clock. Then mounted on a swivel base so it can turn. Incidentally, a cordless radio-clock is an exclusive Bulova feature. The Bulova people figured it all out.

It's very different. But with good reasons.

You're never faced with too many knobs and numbers because Bulova believes in clean, simple design. It's so good looking, we know one man who wakes up at night just to look at it.

And it's cordless. Put it anyplace. There'll be no cord stretching across the room.

All Bulova radio-clocks are small. The Classic (shown above) is only 4½ inches high. Room for more peanut butter sandwiches on your night table. Price... $49.95.

(We know you can get other radio-clocks for less. But maybe they give you less.) **Bulova**

This Bulova cordless electric clock gives you the news.

Because it's also a cordless radio. The world's only completely cordless radio-clock. A tiny transistorized radio. Put back to back to a precision-jeweled clock. Then mounted on a swivel base so it can turn. Incidentally, a cordless radio-clock is an exclusive Bulova feature. The Bulova people figured it all out.

It's very different. But with good reasons. You're never faced with too many knobs and numbers because Bulova believes in clean, simple design. It's so good looking, we know one man who wakes up a night just to look at it.

And it's cordless. Put it anyplace. There'll be no cord stretching across the room.

All Bulova radio-clocks are small. The Classic (shown above) is only $4^1/_2$ inches high. Room for more peanut butter sandwiches on your night table. Price... $49.95.

(We know you can get other radio-clocks for less. But maybe they give you less.)

Advertisement

A Yashica for everyone!

Millions of Yashica cameras have been sold in America... clear evidence of how photographers—from rank beginner to advanced professional—feel about Yashica. There are over 30 cameras and scores of accessories in the line today, in nearly every category: SLR, twin-lens, 35mm rangefinder, half-frame, instant-loading, sub- and ultra miniature, and movie. Prices range from about $34 to $225. There must be one just right for you.

1966 in Cinema and Film

The early '60s in cinema was memorable for many sweeping heroic period films such as *Spartacus* (1960), *Lawrence of Arabia* (1962), *Cleopatra* (1963), *The Greatest Story Ever Told* (1965), and *Doctor Zhivago* (1965). In 1966, three historical epics made the Top 10 Highest Grossing Films list– *Hawaii, The Bible: In the Beginning...* and *The Sand Pebbles*. However, movie studios struggled under the financial burden required by these extravaganzas, and the era of big budget epic movies was coming to an end.

James Mason & Lynn Redgrave in *Georgy Girl*, 1966.

Michael Caine in *Alfie*, 1966.

Riding the wave of the British Invasion, three British films made the Top 10 Highest Grossing list in 1966– *A Man for All Seasons*, and the light-hearted romantic comedies *Alfie* and *Georgy Girl*.

1966 film debuts

Candice Bergen	The Group
Michael Douglas	Cast a Giant Shadow
Harrison Ford	Dead Heat on a Merry-Go-Round
Bette Midler	Hawaii
Helen Mirren	Press for Time

* From en.wikipedia.org/wiki/1966_in_film.

Clint Eastwood as "Blondie" in *The Good, The Bad and The Ugly,* (United Artists, 1966).

To reduce production costs the major studios looked to filming in cheaper locations elsewhere, in particular Britain, Spain and Italy. This was the time of the modern "Spaghetti Westerns"– Italian-made productions starring a host of European actors with fading, or up-and-coming Hollywood stars. Clint Eastwood transitioned from television to cinema with three such films: *A Fistful of Dollars* (1964), *For a Few Dollars More* (1965), and *The Good, The Bad and The Ugly* (1966).

Hollywood also had to compete with rising talent from foreign film directors and foreign stars, such as Brigitte Bardot (France), Sophia Loren (Italy), Sean Connery and Richard Burton (England).

Brigitte Bardot.   Sophia Loren.

Espionage Films of 1966

Agent for H.A.R.M. (Universal Pictures, 1966).

Fantastic Voyage (20th Century Fox, 1966).

Combining thrilling action with exotic locations, a dose of escapism and political intrigue or science fiction, the Spy Genre or Espionage films grew in popularity during the mid-'60s.

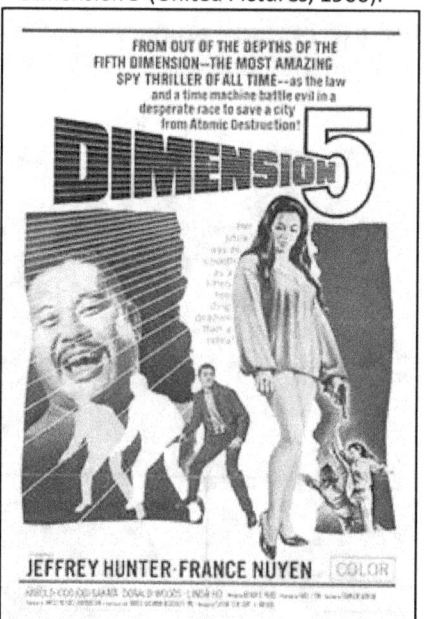

Dimension 5 (United Pictures, 1966).

One Spy Too Many (MGM, 1966).

Top Grossing Films of the Year

1	Hawaii	United Artists	$15,600,000
2	The Bible: In the Beginning...	20th Century Fox	$15,000,000
3	Who's Afraid of Virginia Woolf?	Warner Bros.	$14,500,000
4	The Sand Pebbles	20th Century Fox	$13,500,000
5	A Man for All Seasons	Columbia Pictures	$12,800,000
6	The Russians Are Coming, the Russians Are Coming	United Artists	$9,800,000
7	Grand Prix	MGM	$9,300,000
8	The Professionals	Columbia Pictures	$8,800,000
9	Alfie	Paramount Pictures	$8,500,000
10	Georgy Girl	Columbia Pictures	$7,600,000

* From en.wikipedia.org/wiki/1966_in_film by box office gross in the USA.

The critically acclaimed black comedy-drama *Who's Afraid of Virginia Wolf?* achieved nominations in every category at the Academy Awards. It won five Oscars, including *Best Picture*, and *Best Actress* for Elizabeth Taylor, who gained 30 pounds (13.5kg) for the role.

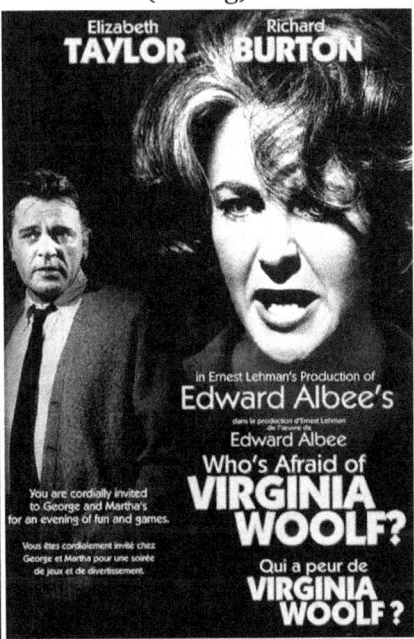

Advertisement

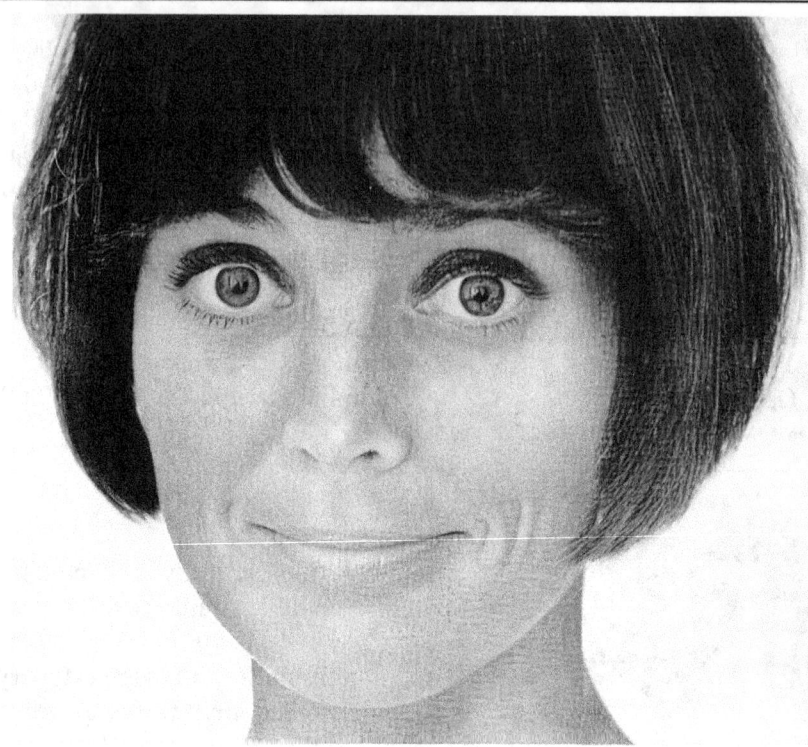

Old Maid.

That's what the other United Air Lines stewardesses call her. Because she's been flying for almost three years now. (The average tenure of a United stewardess is only 21 months before she gets married.)

But she's not worried.

How many girls do you know who can serve cocktails and dinner for 35 without losing their composure? And who smile the whole time like they mean it? (They do.)

Not too many, right? That's part of the reason why only one of every 30 girls who apply for stewardess school makes it.

But still, since United invented the stewardess back in 1930, we've trained over 15,000 smiling reasons to fly the friendly skies.

Maybe that's why more people fly United than any other airline.

Everyone gets warmth, friendliness and extra care. And someone may get a wife.

"Billy, I think you're keen, too. But you're only 8 years old."

fly the friendly skies of United.

Advertisement

Lift the lid...

all controls and changer rise to meet you

in new Admiral "Flight Deck" solid-state stereo

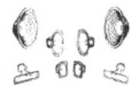

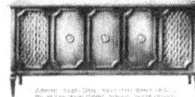

Admiral Stereo

Lift the lid of new Admiral "Flight Deck" solid-state stereo. All controls, including Admiral four-speed record changer, rise to cabinet top level, automatically! Load records, tune FM, AM or FM stereo multiplex radio, with new convenience only Admiral has. The Admiral "Flight Deck" rises a full five inches, the difference between hard-to-reach and easy-to-use!

But convenience is just a prelude to your Admiral music pleasure. Admiral solid-state stereo has up to 360 watts of peak power. Power, to assure you the most realistic stereo reproduction you have ever heard. Power, to re-create every high and low on your stereo records!

Admiral professional-type components give you maximum fidelity, minimum record wear. For example, you can set ideal tracking pressure on the Admiral Vari-Gram Tone Arm—from 0 to 4 grams. The new Admiral solid-state cartridge doesn't depend on delicate record grooves to generate signal strength, as ordinary types do, because it's amplifier-powered. And it's a floating cartridge; even if bumped, it can't scratch you records. They last virtually a lifetime!

Two remarkable new Admiral mid-range speakers are chambered and rear-vented, free of interference from "lows", to give extraordinary new life to important middle-frequency sounds. In addition, Admiral offers two 12" woofers, two $3\frac{1}{2}$" tweeters and two tweeter horns. All eight quality Admiral speakers sound off in a handsome, handcrafted cabinet up to 74 inches long, for magnificent, widespread stereo separation.

If you love music and appreciate convenience, too, enjoy new Admiral "Flight Deck" solid-state stereo. It's the ultimate in stereo!

Musical Memories

For a few short years in the mid-'60s, the youth of the world were clamoring for all things British. This "British Invasion" delivered a flood of British talent to prominence around the world, pushing their music to the top of the charts.

British bands were touring aboard in record numbers, introducing the youth of the world to the unique sounds of the Yardbirds, The Who, The Kinks, Herman's Hermits and The Rolling Stones.

The British Invasion, led by mega-band The Beatles, inspired artists to write their own songs, play their own music, and experiment with exotic sounds. Indian instruments, feedback and distortion, spiced with a good dose of marijuana and LSD, paved the way for psychedelic pop and rock of the late '60s.

The Beatles chose not to tour again after August 1966, marking the end of the crazed fanaticism known as Beatlemania.

Top: The Kinks.
Above: The Beatles.
Left: Petula Clarke.

Petula Clarke was already a seasoned singer and actress when her international hit *Downtown* shot to #1 on the US Billboard Charts. Her next 15 singles made the US top 40, giving her the title "Queen of the British Invasion".

She was a favorite guest of US talk show hosts, even hosting her own TV specials on NBC and ABC. From 1966-1968, she starred in her own TV series *This is Petula Clarke*, for the BBC.

By the end of 1966, American bands were coming into their own. Inspired by the experimental music of the British Invasion, mixed with new psychedelic sounds and feel-good rhythms, The Beach Boys, The Monkeys, Nancy Sinatra, The Mamas & The Papas, and many more acts began to climb the charts. They would soon displace the total British domination of earlier years.

Throughout the decade, unaffected by the impact of the British artists, Motown continued to pump out the hits. This independent record label from Detroit represented top selling artists including The Temptations, The Supremes, Marvin Gaye, Stevie Wonder, Four Tops, and Jackson 5.

Twenty Motown songs would reach #1 on the Billboard Top 100 during the '60s. By bringing the smooth "uptown" R&B and Soul sounds of Black America into the mainstream, Motown remains one of the most influential record labels of the century.

Top: The Beachboys.
Middle: The Temptations.
Right: Jackson 5.

Advertisement

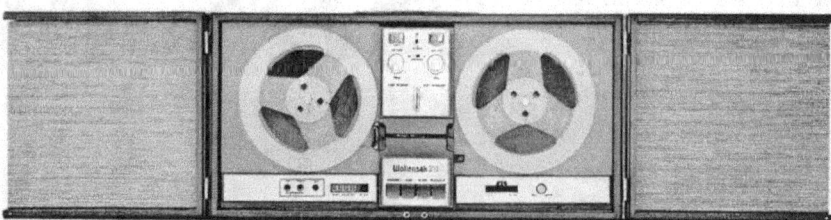

Sophisticated simplicity, with a talent for living...
new Wollensak twin-wing stereo Tape Recorder

Handsome matching speakers in this Wollensak produce true stereo separation... the full, sophisticated sound of music at its best. Speakers swing out for play, fold when not in use. Easily detachable for strategic placement on wall, or table, in bookcase. Control Central groups all controls within a handspan. Solid-state circuitry responds instantly without warmup, plays cool. Vertical or horizontal operation at $7\frac{1}{2}$, $3\frac{3}{4}$, $1\frac{7}{8}$ IPS... a speed for every need. The cabinetry is of hand-finished hardwoods. Attractively woven speaker facings. Trim and metal surfaces are in a muted gold tone. Wollensak quality features: Separate tone and volume control, contoured power push buttons, calibrated dials, two VU meters, 4 digit tape counter. See these stereo Tape Recorders at your Wollensak dealer's. Model 5750 shown large above, $249.95*. Similar models priced from $219.95*. **Wollensak 3M**

Sophisticated simplicity, with a talent for living...
New Wollensak twin-wing stereo Tape Recorder

Handsome matching speakers in the Wollensak produce true stereo separation... the full, sophisticated sound of music at its best. Speakers swing out for play, fold when not in use. Easily detachable for strategic placement on wall, or table, in bookcase. Control Central groups all controls within a handspan. Solid-state circuitry responds instantly without warmup, plays cool. Vertical or horizontal operation at $7\frac{1}{2}$, $3\frac{3}{4}$, $1\frac{7}{8}$, IPS... a speed for every need.

The cabinetry is of hand-finished hardwoods. Attractively woven speaker facings. Trim and metal surfaces are in a muted gold tone. Wollensak quality features: Separate tone and volume control, contoured power push buttons, calibrated dials, two VU meters, 4 digit tape counter. See these stereo Tape Recorders at your Wollensak dealer's. Model 5750 shown large above, $249.95. Similar models priced from $219.95.

Wes Wilson's Psychedelic Concert Posters

The psychedelic posters created by San Francisco artist Wes Wilson spearheaded the hippy aesthetic of flowing lava lamp designs with bubbly lettering in kaleidoscopic colors. Inspired by the freedom of the Art Nouveau, Wilson's ideas for turning posters into expressive artforms were a radical departure from the usual plain and legible poster typography.

During 1966, Wilson created 40 posters for the Fillmore Auditorium in San Francisco, making the venue a focal point for American psychedelic music and countercultures.

Bill Graham presents in San Francisco. Jefferson Airplane, Grateful Dead. Fri. 12 Aug. Sat. 13 Aug. Fillmore Auditorium.

Bill Graham presents in San Francisco. Otis Rush, Grateful Dead, The Canned Heat Blues Band. Fri. Sat. 9pm $3.00. Sun. 2-7pm $2.00. At the Fillmore.

Bill Graham presents in San Francisco. Buffalo Springfield, Steve Miller Blues Band. All Alive at the Fillmore. And Freedom Highway. April 28,29,30.

1966 Billboard Top 30 Songs

	Artist	Song Title
1	The Mamas & the Papas	California Dreamin'
2	? and the Mysterians	96 Tears
3	Jimmy Ruffin	What Becomes of the Brokenhearted
4	The Monkees	Last Train to Clarksville
5	Four Tops	Reach Out I'll Be There
6	Nancy Sinatra	These Boots Are Made for Walkin'
7	The Association	Cherish
8	Frank Sinatra	Strangers in the Night
9	Paul Revere & the Raiders	Kicks
10	Barry Sadler	Ballad of the Green Berets

Four Tops, 1968.

Frank & Nancy Sinatra, 1966.

The Mamas & the Papas, 1967.

The Monkees, 1966.

Artist	Song Title
11 The Young Rascals	Good Lovin'
12 The Righteous Brothers	(You're My) Soul and Inspiration
13 The Supremes	You Can't Hurry Love
14 Bobby Hebb	Sunny
15 The Happenings	See You In September
16 Sam the Sham and the Pharaohs	Li'l Red Riding Hood
17 Lou Christie	Lightnin' Strikes
18 Johnny Rivers	Poor Side of Town
19 Lee Dorsey	Working In The Coal Mine
20 The Mindbenders	A Groovy Kind of Love

The Supremes, 1967.

Donovan, 1965.

21 Dusty Springfield	You Don't Have To Say You Love Me
22 Donovan	Sunshine Superman
23 Sandy Posey	Born a Woman
24 The Mamas & the Papas	Monday, Monday
25 The Cyrkle	Red Rubber Ball
26 Roger Williams	Born Free
27 The Left Banke	Walk Away Renée
28 The Capitols	Cool Jerk
29 Carla Thomas	B-A-B-Y
30 Tommy James and the Shondells	Hanky Panky

* From the *Billboard* top 30 singles of 1966.

Fashion choices from the Montgomery Ward catalog, Summer 1966.

Fashion Trends of the 1960s

The 1960s was an exciting decade for fashion, with new trends that caught on and transformed quickly. It was a decade of fashion extremes driven by shifting social movements, radical youth, rebelliousness and rejection of traditions.

In the early '60s, fashion was content to continue the conservative classic style of the previous decade. The elegant sheath dress and tailored skirt-suits were favored for day wear.

And for dinners and cocktails, '50s style hourglass dresses were still common. Skirts stayed long, full and very lady-like. Matching accessories such as gloves, hat, scarves, jewelry and stiletto or kitten-heel shoes were mandatory.

Jacqueline Kennedy may have been the US first lady for only three years, but as first lady of fashion, her iconic status has endured till this day. Always impeccably groomed, her every move was analyzed and cataloged by newspaper and style magazines for every lady to follow.

Here are some of her classic iconic looks:
- Tailored skirt-suit with three-quarter sleeve length box jacket and matching pill box hat.
- Sheath dress with white gloves and low-heel pump shoes.
- A-line dress, long or short, with three-quarter length gloves for evening.

However, the conservative elegance of the early '60s would soon be energetically and wholeheartedly rejected. The decade of the 1960s belonged to the British youth centered around London, who would capture the world's attention with their free spirits, energy, music, and style. By 1967, the "British Invasion" had exploded on the world, introducing us to the "Mods" and the "Swinging Sixties". These movements defined the era and changed the world of fashion forever.

The Mods were clean-cut college boys who favored slim-fitting suits or short jackets over turtle-neck or buttoned up polo shirts. Pants were pipe-legged with no cuffs, worn over pointed polished shoes or ankle boots.

The Mods were obsessed with Italian fashion, French haircuts, alternative music and Vespa scooters.

Mod fashion was adopted by the many British Invasion bands of the mid-'60s: The Kinks, The Who, The Yardbirds, The Rolling Stones and The Beatles all adopted the Mod look in the early part of their careers.

For the girls, London designer Mary Quant created fashion for the young and free-spirited woman. Credited for inventing the mini-skirt, Quant considered her youthful designs liberating, allowing women to run and move freely. Her clients were hedonistic, creative, wealthy, and sexually liberated. They helped shape the Swinging Sixties cultural revolution.

Quant's Kings Road boutique featured her trademark simple short sheath dresses in bold or floral patterns, worn with solid colored or patterned tights.

She also championed trousers for women– with choices ranging from long flared, harem, or ankle length Capris, to mid-length Bermudas and skimpy hotpants.

Below Left: Mary Quant.
Below Right: Models in Quant plastic coats and boots.

Top: Models wear Mary Quant dresses.
Above: Quant inspired street dresses.

Quant's experimental use of new materials was revolutionary. Shiny PVC raincoats came in an array of solid statement colors, matched with patent vinyl boots. Synthetic dresses paired with a range of bold, colorful plastic jewellery, handbags and accessories.

Advertisement

What do you wear under Actionwear? Actionwear Underwear.

Sears has it. The first inside-outside Actionwear outfit for juniors. Including the new Actionwear bra and panty girdle. The Actionwear underwear is made with Chemstrand Blue "C" spandex. This means you get great comfort plus control. Smoothline seam-free cup bra with stretchy straps, sizes A and B, 32 to 36. About $5. Design-in-Motion panty Girdle, with mesh inserts in back for extra give, 5-15 (junior sizes). About $6. Now you're ready for Actionwear pants (100% stretch Blue "C" nylon) and Actionwear top (50% polyester/50% stretch Blue "C" nylon). Top, S-M-L (junior sizes) about $5. Pants 5-13, about $9. Also in loden and pale blue. And all tagged Actionwear, the very best in stretch clothes. Tested and approved by Chemstrand. So run right now to Sears, Roebuck and Co. That's where the Action is for juniors.

Actionwear. The very best in stretch clothes.

The Swinging Sixties was also the era of the first wave of British supermodels–tall, skinny, leggy young ladies who broke with the aristocratic look of earlier-generation models. With enormous eyes and quirky descriptive names, Jean Shrimpton, Twiggy and Penelope Tree were in-demand icons world-wide.

Penelope Tree for *Vogue,* October 1967.

Twiggy for *Italian Vogue*, July 1967.

Twiggy various photo shoots.

Jean Shrimpton for *Vogue*, Sept 1967.

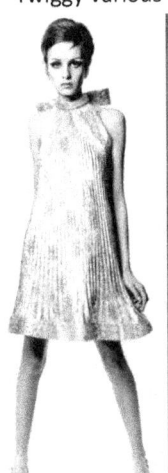

Known as the Space Age designer, French couturier André Courrèges employed geometric shapes in metallic silvers and stark whites to give his dresses futuristic forms. His revolutionary designs from the mid-'60s mixed plastics and fur with leathers and wool, accessorising with astronaut inspired helmets, goggles and flat white go-go boots.

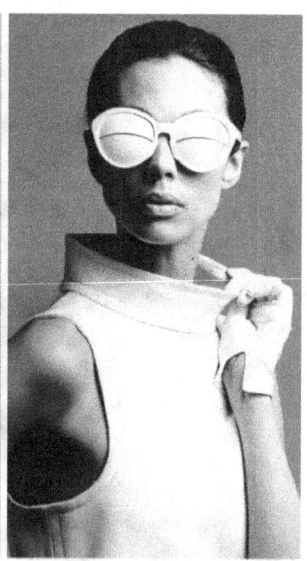

From the Space Age collection of André Courrèges, 1965.

André Courrèges' cut out dress.

Inspired by Courrèges, Space Bride by Jezebel, 1966 New York.

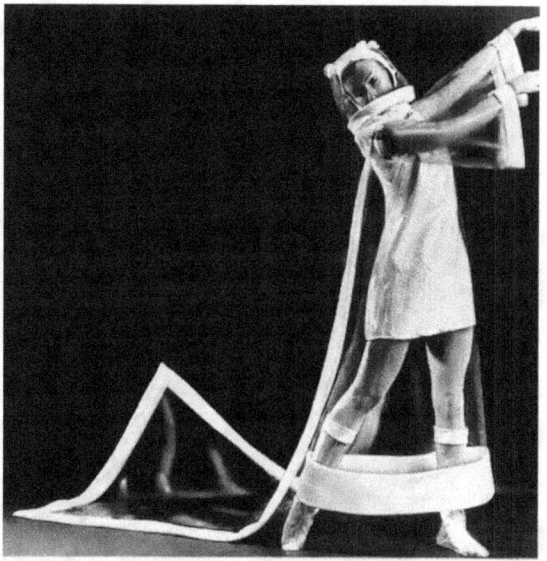

As the fashion and attitudes of swinging London spread to America and other parts of the world, the subculture became commercialized on a mass scale and began to loose its vitality. The fun loving movement morphed into the psychedelic rock and early hippie movements.

Led by musicians such as The Beatles, The Beach Boys, Pink Floyd and The Who, and fuelled by widespread use of marijuana and LSD, psychedelic fashion became an expression of the hallucinogenic experience. Bright colors, swirling patterns and kaleidoscopic floral designs adorned full flowing forms in soft fabrics.

Photo from The Beatles *Magical Mystery Tour,* 1967.

The psychedelic rock movement petered out by the end of the 1960s, but the hippie generation was only just beginning. Hippies would drive fashion forward, well into the next decade.

Advertisement

Do you use artificial sweeteners and still gain weight?

Try putting some sugar into that diet of yours. Seriously!

Sugar fights a primary cause of overweight: overeating. Why?

No other food satisfies hunger so fast with so few calories.

And, sugar gives you the vitality you need to stay active—helps you burn up calories, instead of storing them up as fat.

Sugar's only aftertaste is energy.

Sugar helps diets work

...18 calories per teaspoon— and it's all energy.

Artificial Sweeteners?
"There is no clear justification for the use of artificial sweeteners by the general public as a weight-reducing procedure . . ." (*Food and Nutrition Board of the National Academy of Sciences— National Research Council.*)

Sugar Information, Inc. P.O. Box 2664, Grand Central Station, New York, New York 10017

Do you use artificial sweeteners and still gain weight?
Try putting some sugar into that diet of yours. Seriously!
Sugar fights a primary cause of overweight: overeating. Why?
No other food satisfies hunger so fast with so few calories.
And, sugar gives you the vitality you need to stay active–helps you burn up calories, instead of storing them up as fat.
Sugar's only aftertaste is energy.

Sugar helps diets work...18 calories per teaspoon–and it's all energy.

Artificial Sweeteners? "There is no clear justification for the use of artificial sweeteners by the general public as a weight-reducing procedure..." (Food and Nutrition Board of the National Academy of Sciences–National Research Council.)

Science and Medicine

2nd May– Scottish inventor James Goodfellow patented his inventions for an automated teller machine (ATM) and Personal Identification Number (PIN) technology using an encrypted plastic card. For his inventions, which are still in daily use worldwide, Goodfellow received a £10 bonus from his employer.

30th May– The US states of Nevada and California signed bills into law declaring the psychedelic drug lysergic acid diethylamide (LSD) illegal. Other states would do likewise in the following years. LSD had become the drug of choice for academics, artists, writers and musicians, who advocated the drug's power to increase consciousness.

5th Oct– The Fermi 1 nuclear reactor at Lake Erie, Michigan, suffered a partial fuel meltdown. Core temperature alarms sounded when an unknown blockage caused insufficient coolant to enter the fuel assembly, resulting in several fuel rods reaching dangerously high temperatures and causing them to melt. After repairs, the reactor operated from 1970-1972 before being permanently shut and decommissioned.

Hewlett-Packard (HP) entered the computer market with its compact HP 2116A, the world's first 'plug-and-play' computer. The 2116A was designed for laboratory use, able to interface with a wide array of standard laboratory instruments.

Television engineer Ralph Baer designs the world's first TV games, which could be played on a standard TV without a computer. His "Brown Box" gave the user access to several games, including a table tennis game (a precursor to Atari's Pong).

Advertisement

Whenever you want to go to the Caribbean, just raise your hand.

Better still, give us a call. We have more flights to more of the islands you want than anyone else. And our fares are low. For example, a round-trip 17-day Jet Economy ticket from New York to Jamaica is just $155. As little as that to fly away to a lush, warm, inviting new world. So let us take you there.

To Puerto Rico, possibly, where the rhythm is Spanish and the sun shines 363 days a year. Or St. Thomas, where the pace is rather torrid and the amenities rather deluxe. Or Martinique, where the trade-winds whisper in French. Or Barbados, where the English go native and the natives speak English.

We go to 15 islands in all, so take your choice. And leave the details to any Pan Am Travel Agent or the closest Pan Am office. Wherever we take you, you'll enjoy the good feeling that comes from flying the very best there is. That's easy to take, too.

World's most experienced airline

First in Latin America   First on the Atlantic   First 'Round the World   First on the Pacific

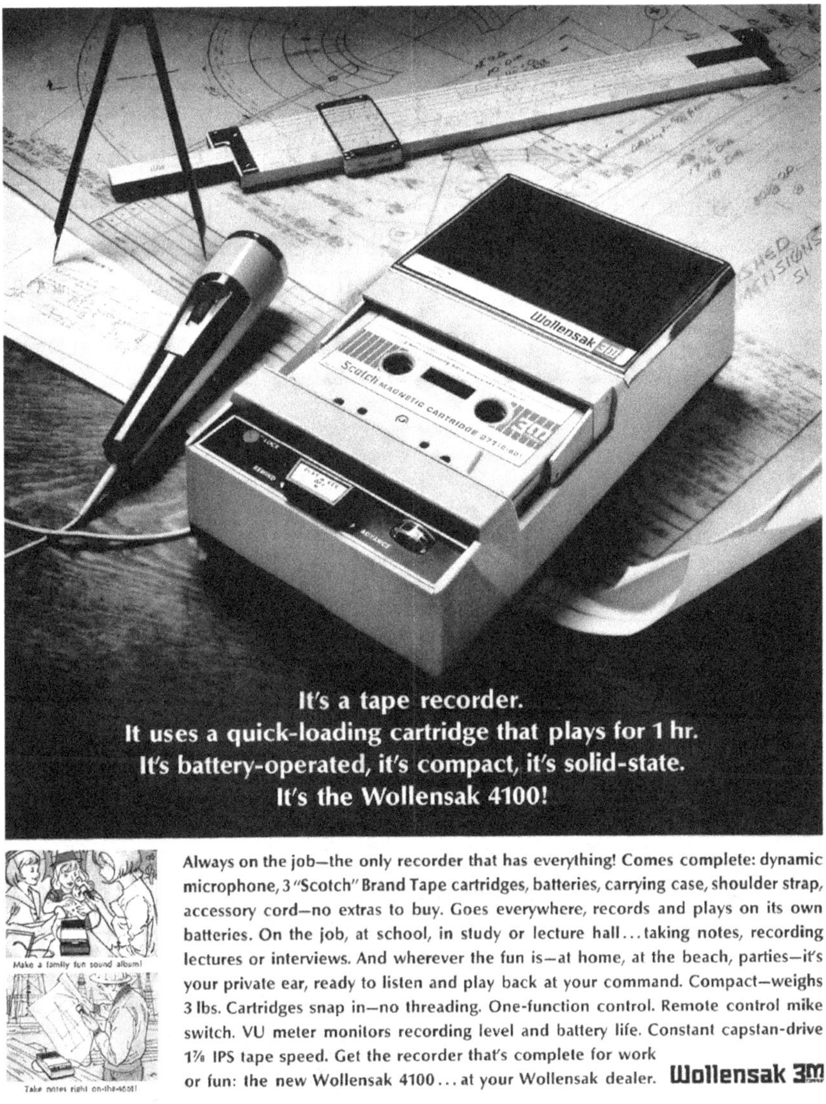

Advertisement

It's a tape recorder.
It uses a quick-loading cartridge that plays for 1 hr.
It's battery-operated, it's compact, it's solid-state.
It's the Wollensak 4100!

Make a family fun sound album! Take notes right on-the-spot!

Always on the job—the only recorder that has everything! Comes complete: dynamic microphone, 3 "Scotch" Brand Tape cartridges, batteries, carrying case, shoulder strap, accessory cord—no extras to buy. Goes everywhere, records and plays on its own batteries. On the job, at school, in study or lecture hall...taking notes, recording lectures or interviews. And wherever the fun is—at home, at the beach, parties—it's your private ear, ready to listen and play back at your command. Compact—weighs 3 lbs. Cartridges snap in—no threading. One-function control. Remote control mike switch. VU meter monitors recording level and battery life. Constant capstan-drive 1⅞ IPS tape speed. Get the recorder that's complete for work or fun: the new Wollensak 4100... at your Wollensak dealer. **Wollensak 3M**

It's a tape recorder. It uses a quick-loading cartridge that plays for 1 hr. It's battery-operated, it's compact, it's solid-state. It's the Wollensak 4100!

Make a family fun sound album! Take notes right on-the-spot!
Always on the job–the only recorder that has everything! Comes complete: dynamic microphone, 3 "Scotch" Brand Tape cartridges, batteries, carrying case, shoulder strap, accessory cord—no extras to buy. Goes everywhere, records and plays on its own batteries. On the job, at school, in study or lecture hall...taking notes, recording lectures or interviews. And wherever the fun is—at home, at the beach, parties—it's your private ear, ready to listen and play back at your command. Compact—weighs 3lbs. Cartridges snap in—no threading. One-function control. Remote control mike switch. VU meter monitors recording level and battery life. Constant capstand-drive $1^7/_8$ IPS tape speed. Get the recorder that's complete for work or fun: the new Wollensak 4100...at your Wollensak dealer.

VIII British Empire & Commonwealth Games

The 1966 *British Empire and Commonwealth Games* (later known as *The Commonwealth Games*) were held in Kingston, Jamaica from 4th-13th August. It would be the first time a non-white nation, and the only time a Caribbean country, would host the Games.

Despite concerns about the small country's limited infrastructure and resources, Jamaica succeeded in building the venues, and surpassed all expectations with its presentation and organization of the Games.

Jim Alder (Scotland) wins Marathon gold. Only eight runners survived the Caribbean heat to finish.

34 nations competed in 9 events, with England winning the most medals (80 medals including 33 gold). Australia came second (73 medals including 23 gold).

As was the tradition, England, Scotland, Wales, and Northern Ireland competed separately.

The Games were officially opened by HRH Prince Philip, the Duke of Edinburgh. He was accompanied by a young Prince Charles (17 yrs old), and Princess Anne (14 yrs old).

Imperial measurements were used for the last time, as the switch to metric would be made for next Games in 1970.

Prince Philip receives the Queen's baton from Jamaican Keith Gardner at the Opening Ceremony.

Also in Sports

9th Mar– Muhammad Ali was drafted by the United States military. As a conscientious objector he would later refuse to sign up. Ali was convicted of draft refusal and sentenced to five years imprisonment, although he remained free during the ongoing appeals process. In 1971 the US Supreme Court overturned his conviction.

22nd May-23rd Oct– Australian Jack Brabham won the F1 Driver's Championship for the third time, one of only 10 drivers to have achieved 3 wins.

2nd Jul– Young rising American tennis star Billie Jean King won the first of her 12 Grand Slam Women's Singles titles, beating Maria Bueno of Brazil 6-3, 3-6, 6-1 at Wimbledon.

9th Jul– Jack Nicklaus became the 4th person in history to win all 4 majors (Career Grand Slam) when he won the British Open Men's Golf in Muirfield. He would repeat this feat in 1971 and 1978.

30th Jul– Thirty-two million TV viewers watched England beat West Germany 4-2 to win the FIFA World Cup at Wembley, UK.

11th-25th Jul– The 10th Central American & Caribbean Games were held in San Juan, Puerto Rico. 1,689 athletes from 18 countries participated.

9th-20th Dec– The 5th Asian Games were held in Bangkok, Thailand. 2,500 athletes and officials from 18 countries participated.

Other News from 1966

19th Jan– Indira Gandhi was elected India's 4th Prime Minister. She became the first woman to lead the country, serving from 1966 to March 1977, and from January 1980 until her assassination in October 1984.

14th Feb– Australia switched to the decimal currency.

31st Mar– Prime Minister Harold Wilson led the British Labour Party to a general election win with a landslide majority of 96 seats. Wilson had already been PM for 17 months, with an unworkable lead of only 4 seats.

16th May– Mao Zedong launched China's Cultural Revolution, calling for violent class struggle to rid the country of capitalist influences. Estimates of up to 20 million deaths would occur over the next 10 years through persecution, massacres, torture, and suicide. Over 10 million intellectuals and scholars were forced to "retrain" as farmers.

1st Jul– Medicare commenced in the USA to benefit the elderly and disabled regardless of race, income or medical history.

13th Jul– The Hare Krishna movement was founded in New York City by A. C. Bhaktivedanta Swami Prabhupada.

15th Sep– US President Lyndon B. Johnson wrote to Congress urging the enactment of gun control legislation.

26th Oct– NATO moved from Paris to Brussels following France's decision to remove French troops from NATO and to close all bases and HQs.

8th Nov– Edward W. Brooke (Rep-R-Mass) became the 1st African American popularly elected to the US Senate.

8th Nov– Actor and TV personality Ronald Reagan was elected Governor of California.

24th Nov– Severe smog in New York City caused the deaths of 400 people from respiratory failure & heart attack.

15th Nov– Walt Disney died of lung cancer. He had been a pack-a-day smoker.

26th May-4th Oct– Botswana, Lesotho, and Guyana became independent states within the British Commonwealth.

In Aviation:

– An Air India Boeing-707 plane crashed into Mont Blanc, France, killing 117 (24th Jan).

– An All-Nippon Airways 727 plane crashed off Haneda Airport, Japan, killing 133 (4th Feb).

– BOAC Flight 911 crashed over Mt Fuji, Japan, killing 124 (5th March).

– A Britannia Airways Flight 105 crashed in Ljubljana, Yugoslavia, killing 98 British tourists (1st Sept).

Famous People Born in 1966

13th Jan– Patrick Dempsey, American actor.

19th Jan– Stefan Edberg, Swedish tennis player.

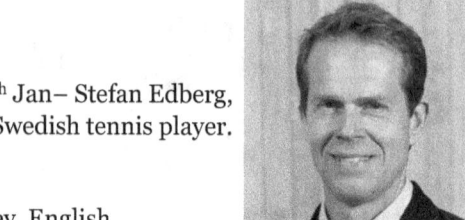

6th Feb– Rick Astley, English singer & songwriter.

7th Feb– Chris Rock, American comedian & actor.

20th Feb– Cindy Crawford, American model, actress & businesswoman

24th Feb– Billy Zane, American actor.

1st Mar– Paul Hollywood, English baker & TV judge.

6th Mar– Alan Davies, British comedian & actor.

8th Apr– Robin Wright, American actress.

9th Apr– Cynthia Nixon, American actress.

14th Apr– Greg Maddux, American Baseball pitcher (Hall of Fame).

16th May– Janet Jackson, American singer.

23rd May– Graeme Hick MBE, English cricket batsman.

26th May– Helena Bonham Carter, British actress.

21st Jun– Gretchen Carlson, American TV commentator.

27th Jun– J. J. Abrams, American writer, producer & director.

28th Jun– John Cusack, American actor.

30th Jun– Mike Tyson, American boxer.

1st Jul– Patrick McEnroe, American tennis player, coach & broadcaster.

14th Aug– Halle Berry, American actress.

2nd Sep– Salma Hayek, Mexican-American actress.

9th Sep– Adam Sandler, American actor & comedian.

11th Sep– Princess Akishino, Japanese Imperial Family.

9th Oct– David Cameron, British Prime Minister (Conservative: 2010-16).

11th Oct– Luke Perry, American actor (d.2019).

17th Oct– Doug McMillon, American CEO of Wal-Mart Stores, Inc. (2014-).

2nd Nov– David Schwimmer, American actor.

7th Nov– Calvin Borel, American jockey (Racing Hall of Fame).

8th Nov– Gordon Ramsay, British chef & TV personality.

17th Jeff Buckley, American musician & singer (d. 1997).

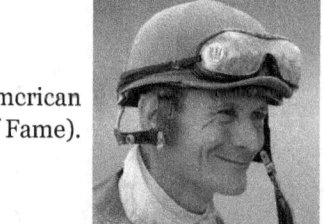

17th Nov– Kate Ceberano, Australian singer.

21st Nov– Troy Aikman, American footballer & broadcaster (Hall of Fame).

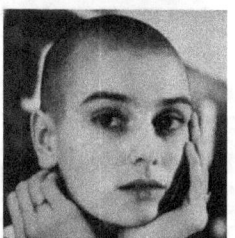

8th Dec– Sinead O'Connor, Irish singer-songwriter (d.2023).

Advertisement

More and More People Prefer Miller High Life
During the entertaining season, treat your friends to the very best with mellow
Miller High Life... always in good taste!
Sparkling... Flavorful... Distinctive!
The Champagne of Bottle Beer

1966 in Numbers

Census Statistics [1]

- Population of the world   3.41 billion
- Population in the United States   201.9 million
- Population in the United Kingdom   54.57 million
- Population in Canada   19.98 million
- Population in Australia   11.59 million
- Average age for marriage of women   20.5 years old
- Average age for marriage of men   22.8 years old
- Average family income USA $7,400 per year
- Minimum wage USA $1.25 per hour

Costs of Goods [2]

- Average home — $20,705
- Average new car — $2,650
- New Triumph TR6 — $3,275
- A gallon of gasoline — $0.31
- Margarine — $0.31 per pound
- A gallon of milk — $0.97
- Loaf of bread — $0.18
- Porterhouse steak — $1.19 per pound
- Bacon — $0.79 per pound
- Sweet corn — $0.05 each
- Fresh eggs — $0.55 per dozen
- Potatoes — $0.37 per 5 pounds
- Heinz Ketchup — $0.22
- Kraft processed cheese — $0.39 for 8 oz

---

[1] Figures taken from worldometers.info/world-population, US National Center for Health Statistics, Divorce and Divorce Rates US (cdc.gov/nchs/data/series/sr_21/sr21_029.pdf) and US Census Bureau, Historical Marital Status Tables (census.gov/data/tables/time-series/demo/families/marital.html).
[2] From thepeoplehistory.com, mclib.info/reference/local-history & dqydj.com/historical-home-prices/.

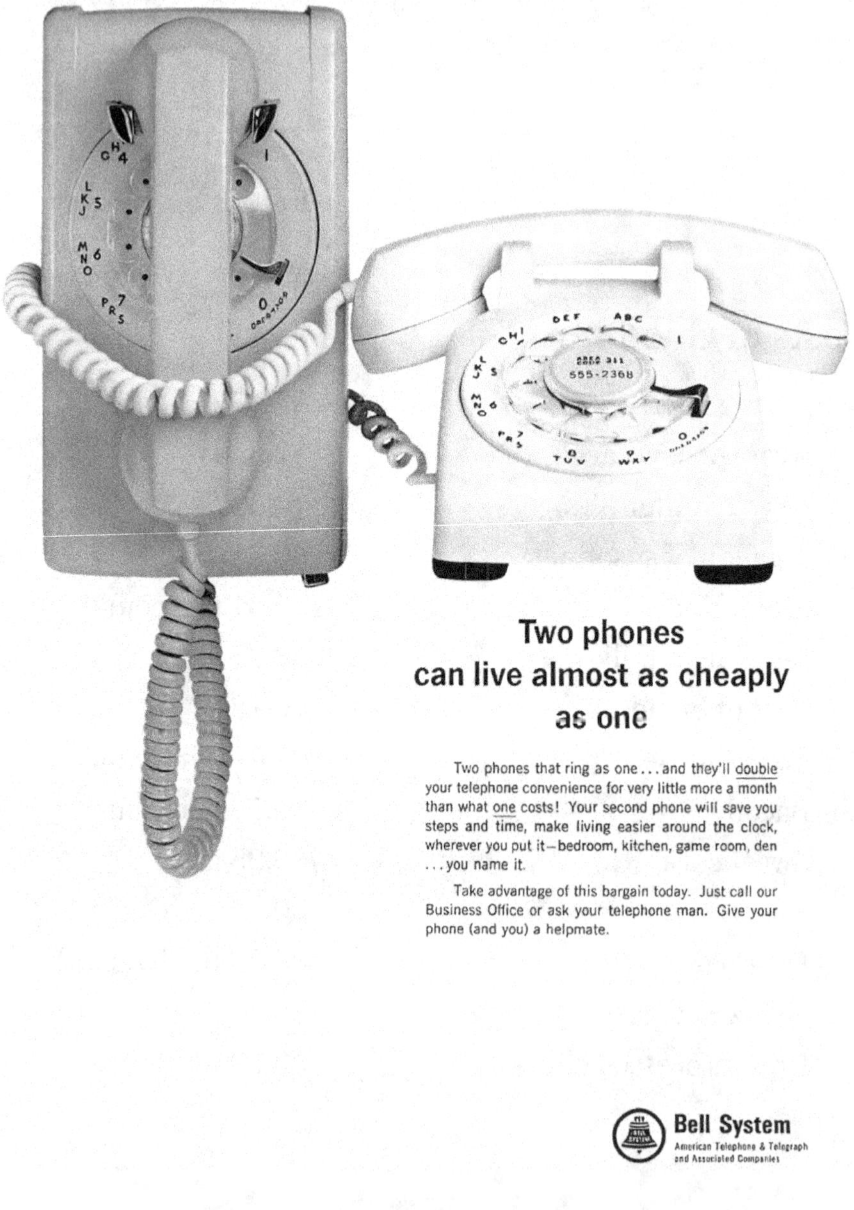

Advertisement

Two phones can live almost as cheaply as one

Two phones that ring as one... and they'll double your telephone convenience for very little more a month than what one costs! Your second phone will save you steps and time, make living easier around the clock, wherever you put it—bedroom, kitchen, game room, den ...you name it.

Take advantage of this bargain today. Just call our Business Office or ask your telephone man. Give your phone (and you) a helpmate.

Bell System
American Telephone & Telegraph
and Associated Companies

Two phones can live almost as cheaply as one

Two phones that ring as one... and they'll double your telephone convenience for very little more a month than what one costs! Your second phone will save you steps and time, make living easier around the clock, wherever you put it– bedroom, kitchen, game room, den... you name it.

Take advantage of this bargain today. Just call our Business Office or ask your telephone man. Give your phone (and you) a helpmate.

Advertisement

Who's drinking all that Diet-Rite Cola?

Everybody!

Diet-Rite is the new family favorite of millions—the best-tasting cola you can buy. Better-tasting than old-time favorites...or their low-calorie offshoots. No sugar at all. Less than 1 calorie per bottle. Bring home a carton of Diet-Rite Cola for your family...today!

America's no.1 low-calorie cola

Who's drinking all that Diet-Rite Cola?
Everybody!

Diet-Rite is the new family favorite of millions—the best-tasting cola you can buy. Better-tasting than old-time favorites...or their low-calorie offshoots. No sugar at all. Less than 1 calorie per bottle. Bring home a carton of Diet-Rite Cola for your family...today!

America's no.1 low-calorie cola

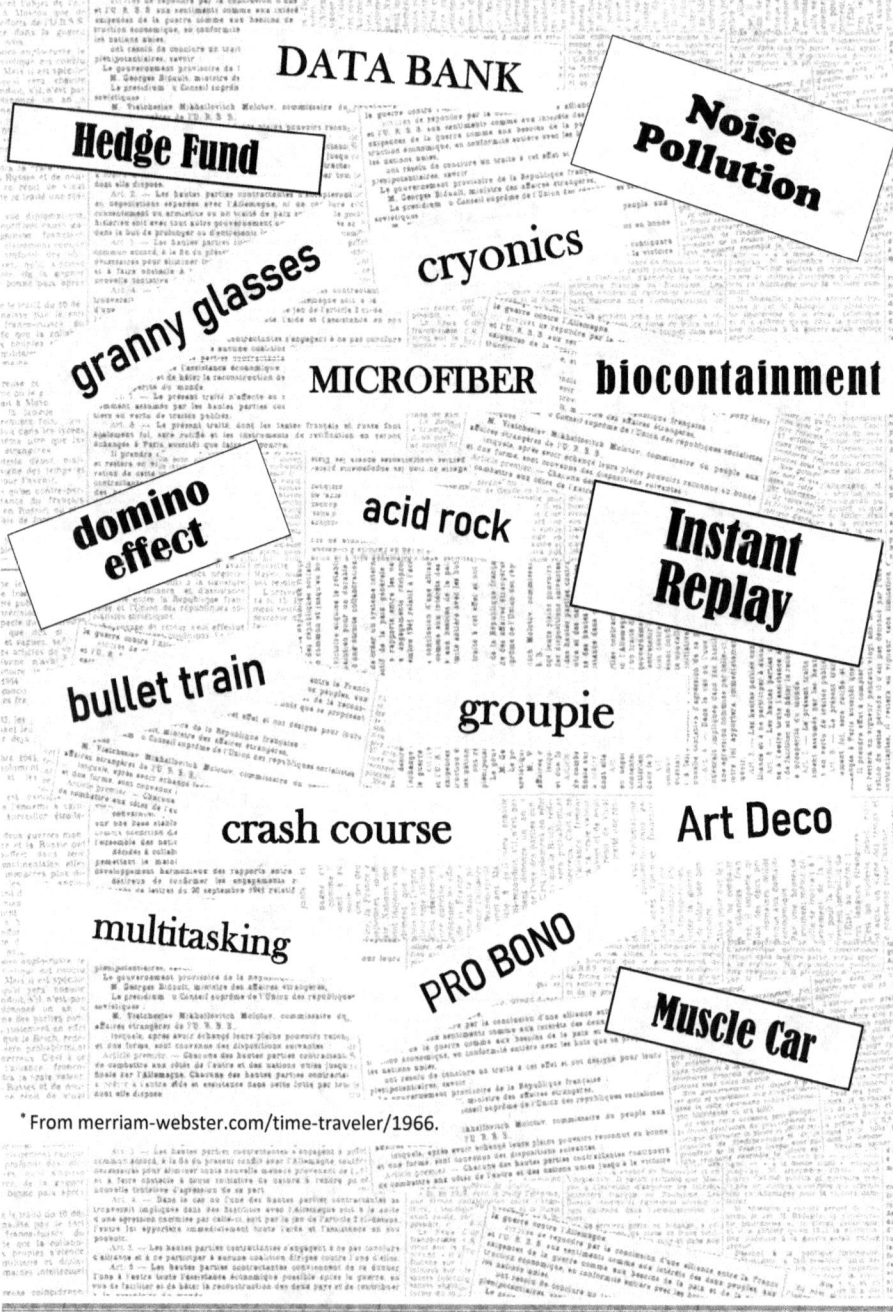

A heartfelt plea from the author:

I sincerely hope you enjoyed reading this book and that it brought back many fond memories from the past.

Success as an author has become increasingly difficult with the proliferation of **AI generated** copycat books by unscrupulous sellers. They are clever enough to escape copyright action and use dark web tactics to secure paid-for **fake reviews**, something I would never do.

Hence I would like to ask you—I plead with you—the reader, to leave a star rating or review on Amazon. This helps make my book discoverable for new readers, and helps me to compete fairly against the devious copycats.

If this book was a gift to you, you can leave stars or a review on your own Amazon account, or you can ask the gift-giver or a family member to do this on your behalf.

I have enjoyed researching and writing this book for you and would greatly appreciate your feedback.

Best regards,
Bernard Bradforsand-Tyler.

Please leave a book review/rating at:

https://bit.ly/1966-reviews

Or scan the QR code:

Flashback books make the perfect gift- see the full range at

https://bit.ly/FlashbackSeries

Image Attributions

Photographs and images used in this book are reproduced courtesy of the following:

Page 6 – From *Life* mag 8th Apr 1966. Source: books.google.com/books?id=9VUEAAAAMBAJ&printsec. (PD image).*
Page 8 – Advert source: flickr.com/photos/nesster/15007179116/ by Neester. Attribution 4.0 Internat (CC BY 4.0).
Page 9 – Image by Edison Electric Institute, from *Life* magazine 21st Jan 1966. Source: books.google.com/books?id=B0wEAAAAMBAJ&printsec. (PD image).*
Page 10 – Rolling Stones in 1965, source: guitarnoise.com/lessons/play-with-fire/. Creator unknown. – Fans at Shea Stadium, source: vintag.es/2016/03/1965-shea-stadium-beatles-biggest.html. Pre 1978, no mark (PD image).
– Connery, source: flickr.com/photos/slightlyterrific/5380276160 by kate gabrielle. Attribution 4.0 Int (CC BY 4.0).
Page 11 – March Against Fear, creator unknown. Source: time.graphics/period/142044. Pre 1978 (PD image).
Page 12 – From *Life* mag 10th June 1966. Source: books.google.com/books?id=rIUEAAAAMBAJ&printsec. (PD image).*
Page 13 – Carnaby Street, London UK, photo from 1966. Source: standard.co.uk/lifestyle/london-life/26-amazing-photos-of-carnaby-street-in-the-swinging-sixties-and-seventies-a3263291.html.
Page 14 – The Who promotional photo, creator unknown. – Rolling Stones in concert, Sweden, 3rd April 1966 by Ingen Uppgift. Source: commons.wikimedia.org/wiki/File:Kungliga_Tennishallen_Stones_1966a.jpg.
– The Beatles signed photo, source: freeclassicimages.com/images/beatles_autograph.jpg. – Quant dresses, source: https://en.wikipedia.org/wiki/Miniskirt. All images this page pre-1978, no copyright mark (PD image).
Page 15 – Jean Shrimpton, source: search.aol.com/aol/image;_ylt=AwrT4R.VDDZfcdQAiEdjCWVH?q=jean+shrimpton.
– Twiggy, source: search.aol.com/aol/image;_ylt=Awr9DWs_DzZf1qwAvCtjCWVH?q=twiggy&imgl=fsuc&fr2=p%3As%2C v%3Ai. Pre-1978, no copyright mark (PD images). – Book covers** for: *The Whip Hand* by Victor Canning and *The Looking Glass War* by John Le Carre. – Film posters** for: *Gregory Girl*, by Columbia Pictures, and *Alfie* by Paramount Pictures.
Page 16 – From *Life* mag 22nd Jan 1965. Source: books.google.com/books?id=x0gEAAAAMBAJ&printsec. (PD image).*
Page 17 – Rockers, Mods and ladies group photo. Creators unknown. Pre-1978, no copyright mark (PD image).
Page 18 – From *Newsweek* 1st Nov 1965. Source: flickr.com/photos/91591049@N00/20654718988/ by SenseiAlan. Attribution 4.0 International (CC BY 4.0).
Page 19 – Traffic photos from the '60s, from private unknown sources. Pre-1978, no copyright mark (PD image).
Page 20 – From *Life* mag 4th Nov 1966. Source: books.google.com/books?id=EFMEAAAAMBAJ&printsec. (PD image).*
Page 21 – Pontiac, source: flickr.com/photos/91591049@N00/49836566403/. Attribution 4.0 Internat (CC BY 4.0).
– Chrysler, source: blog.consumerguide.com/model-year-madness-10-classic-ads-from-1966/. Pre-1978(PD image).
– 1965 *Unsafe at Any Speed* dustcover, source: en.wikipedia.org/wiki/Unsafe_at_Any_Speed reproduced in low resolution under fair use terms to illustrate the article only.
Page 22 – 1966 Mazda 800, source: flickr.com/photos/aussie-car-adverts/39195841294. Attribute 4.0 Int (CC BY 4.0).
– Datsun, source: ebay.com. Pre-1978, no copyright mark (PD image) –1966 Honda S 600 promotional poster. Source: pinterest.ca/pin/574209021234450633/. Pre-1978, no copyright mark (PD image).
Page 23 – From *Life* mag 6th May 1966. Source: books.google.com/books?id=F1YEAAAAMBAJ&printsec. (PD image).*
Page 24 – From *Life* mag 11th Feb 1966. Source: books.google.com/books?id=JUwEAAAAMBAJ&printsec. (PD image).*
Page 25 – Image from Magnavox advertisement, source: imgur.com/gallery/C2E0x. (PD image).*
Page 26 – Screen still from *The Lucy Show*, 7th Jan 1963, by Desilu Productions.** Source: commons.wikimedia.org/wiki/File:Vivian_Vance_Lucille_Ball_The_Lucy_Show_1963.jpg. – *Green Acres* by CBS Television.** Source: clickamericana.com/ media/television-shows/green-acres-theme-song-lyrics-1965-1971. – Bewitched publicity photo, 1964, by Ashmont Productions. Source: ar.m.wikipedia.org/wiki/:ﻑﻠﻣ-Bewitched_cast_1964.jpg (PD image).
Page 27 – *Star Trek*, screen still 12th Jan 1968, by NBC Television.** Source: en.wikipedia.org/wiki/Star_Trek:_The_Original_Series. – *Mission Impossible*, screen still from 17th Sept 1966, by CBS Television.** Source: en.wikipedia.org/wiki/ Mission_Impossible_(1966_TV_series). – *Daktari* screen still, 11th Feb 1966 by CBS TV.** Source: commons. wikimedia.org/wiki/File:Marshall_Thompson_and_Judy_Daktari_1966.JPG. – *Family Affair*, circa 1967 by CBS Television.** Source: en.wikipedia.org/wiki/Family_Affair#/media/File:Family_affair_1967.JPG.
Page 28 – From *Life* mag 7th Oct 1966. Source: books.google.com/books?id=jFYEAAAAMBAJ&printsec (PD image).*
Page 29 – From *Life* mag 7th Jan 1966. Source: books.google.com/books?id=CkwEAAAAMBAJ&printsec (PD image).*
Page 30 – Nevada bomb test, creator unknown. Source: scarc.library.oregonstate.edu/omeka/items/show/1501.
Page 31 – Gagarin source: tass.com/society/899827 by Valentin Cheredintsev. – Tereshkova: cultura.biografieonline.it/la-prima-donna-nello-spazio/. – Leonov: space.com/alexei-leonov-bio.html. All pre-1978 (PD images).
Page 32 – From *Life* mag 15th Apr 1966. Source: books.google.com/books?id=-VUEAAAAMBAJ&printsec. (PD image).*
Page 33 – Gemini 4 & 8 and Apollo 11 archival images courtesy of nasa.gov/multimedia/imagegallery. All PD images.
Page 34 – Members of the 2nd Battalion, 14th Infantry Regiment, South Vietnam 1966. Image by James K. F. Dung, SFC, photographer, courtesy of the National Archives and Records Administration Identifier (NAID) 530610. Source: enwikipedia.org/ wiki/Bell_UH-1_Iroquois#/media/File:UH-1D_helicopters_in_Vietnam_ 1966.jpg (PD image). – Anti-tank vehicles on Chu Lai beach, June 1965, archival image courtesy of US Department of State prev. USIA. (PD image).

Page 35 – USAF A-37 light attack aircraft by US Air Force, source: museumsyndicate.com/item.php?item= 79632. – Protests sources: wallpaperswide.com/war_protest-wallpapers.html. – texashillcountry.com/life-lyndon-b-johnson-nutshell/. – peacehistory-usfp.org/vietnam-war/. All pre-1978 (PD images).
Page 36 – Hough riots, creator unknown. Pre-1978, no copyright mark (PD image). – MLK addresses crowds at Englewood, 5th Aug 1966, and white counter-protestors at Marquette Park. Both images by Chicago Tribune. Source: chicagomag.com/ Chicago-Magazine/August-2016/Martin-Luther-King-Chicago-Freedom-Movement/.
Page 37 – Division street riots, creator unknown. Pre-1978, no copyright mark (PD image).
– Sunset Strip riots, creator unknown. Pre-1978, no copyright mark (PD image).
Page 38 – From *Life* mag 14th Oct 1966. Source: books.google.com/books?id=IFYEAAAAMBAJ&printsec. (PD image).*
Page 39 – From *Life* mag 3rd Sept 1965. Source: books.google.com/books?id=nVIEAAAAMBAJ&printsec. (PD image).*
Page 40 – Aberfan After Coal Avalanche, 1st Oct 1966. Photo by Terence Spencer/The LIFE Picture Collection. Object name: 20410858.jpg. This image is significant to the article created and is for information only, reproduced under fair use terms. There is no free version available. The image is rendered in low resolution to avoid piracy. It is believed this image will not in any way limit the ability of the copyright owner to market or sell their product.
Page 41 – Verwoerd, source: commons.wikimedia.org/wiki/Category:Hendrik_Frensch_Verwoerd.
– Signage, source: commons.wikimedia.org/wiki/Category:Apartheid_signage. All pre 1978 (PD images).
Page 42 – From *Life* mag 9th Dec 1966. Source: books.google.com/books?id=BlMEAAAAMBAJ&printsec. (PD image).*
Page 43 – Advertisement original creator unknown. Source: flickr.com/photos/80682954@N00/7272378734 by Neester. Attribution 4.0 International (CC BY 4.0).
Page 44 – Georgy Girl publicity still by Columbia Pictures.**
Source: moviestillsdb.com/movies/georgy-girl-i60453/8Yf8Vn.
Page 45 – Michael Caine publicity photo for Alfie by Paramount Pictures.** Source: bamfstyle.com/tag/alfie-1966/.
– Cropped still image from The Good, The Bad and The Ugly by Produzioni Europee Associati / United Artists.**
– Bridgitte Bardot, source: flickr.com/photos/classicvintage/9274563680. Attribution 4.0 International (CC BY 4.0).
– Sophia Loren, source: commons.wikimedia.org/wiki/Category:Sophia_Loren_in_1962. Pre-1978 (PD image).
Page 46 – *Agent for H.A.R.M.* movie poster, 1966, by Universal Pictures.** Source: en.wikipedia.org/wiki/Agent_for_H.A.R.M. – *Fantastic Voyage* movie poster, 1966, by 20th Century Fox.** Source: en.wikipedia.org/wiki/Fantastic_Voyage. – *Dimension 5* movie poster, 1966, by United Pictures.** Source: en.wikipedia.org/wiki/Dimension_5_(film). – *One Spy Too Many* movie poster, 1966, by MGM.** Source: en.wikipedia.org/wiki/One_Spy_Too_Many.
Page 47 – *Hawaii* movie poster, 1966, by United Artists.** Source: en.wikipedia.org/wiki/Hawaii_(1966_film).
– *The Bible: In the Beginning...* movie poster, 1966, by 20th Century Fox.** Source: tvtropes.org/pmwiki/pmwiki.php/Film/TheBible1966. – *Who's Afraid of Virginia Woolf?* movie poster, 1966, by Warner Brothers.**
Source: mycast.io/stories/who-s-afraid-of-virginia-woolf1.
Page 48 – From *Life* mag 11th Nov 1966. Source: books.google.com/books?id=D1MEAAAAMBAJ&printsec (PD image).*
Page 49 – From *Life* mag 14th Oct 1966. Source: books.google.com/books?id=IFYEAAAAMBAJ&printsec. (PD image).*
Page 50 – The Kinks promotional photo, 2nd Sept 1965, creator unknown. Source: en.wikipedia.org/wiki/The_Kinks. (PD image). – The Beatles, creator unknown. Source: flickr.com/photos/beatlesmaniac11/4191790770. Attribution 4.0 International (CC BY 4.0). – Petula Clarke from *Les Plus Grands Succès De Petula Clark*, by Sony. This image is reproduced under Fair Use terms, rendered in low resolution to avoid piracy. It is believed this use will not in any way limit the ability of the copyright owners to sell their product.
Page 51 – The Beachboys 1967 press photo by Capitol Records. Source: commons.wikimedia.org/wiki/Category: Group_photographs_of_the_Beach_Boys#/media/File:Beach_Boys_1967.jpg. – The Temptations promotional photo by Mowtown Records. Source: commons.wikimedia.org/wiki/Category:The_Temptations#/media/File:The_Temptations_1968.JPG. – Jackson 5 announcing their appearance on The Ed Sullivan Show in 1969. Source: commons.wikimedia.org/wiki/Category: The_Jackson_5#/media/File: Jackson_5_1969.jpg. All images this page pre-1978, no copyright mark (PD image).
Page 52 – From *Life* mag 4th Nov 1966. Source: books.google.com/books?id=EFMEAAAAMBAJ&printsec (PD* image)
Page 53 – Concert posters** from USA Library of Congress. Control Numbers: 95504681, 92517368 & 2014647489 (PD images).
Page 54 – The Four Tops, source: commons.wikimedia.org/wiki/File:Grand_Gala_du_Disque_._The_Four_Tops,_Bestanddeelnr_921-1506.jpg 8th Mar 1968, by Ron Kroon / Anefo, from the Nationaal Archief, Dutch National Archives (PD image). – Frank and Nancy Sinatra for CBS Television in 1966,** source: commons.wikimedia.org/wiki/Category: Nancy_Sinatra#/media/File:Frank_and_Nancy_Sinatra_1966.jpg. – The Mamas & the Papas from the ABC TV program, *The Songmakers*, 26th Jan 1967.** – The Monkees publicity photo, 15th Sep 1966, for NBC Television. Source: commons. wikimedia.org/wiki/Category:The_Monkees#/media/File:The_Monkees_1966.JPG. Pre 1978 (PD image).
Page 55 – The Supremes publicity photo by General Artists Corporation from 22nd Dec 1967.
Source: commons.wikimedia. org/ wiki/Category:The_Supremes#/media/File:The_Supremes_1967.JPG. (PD).
– Donovan, 12th July 1965, by Nijs, Jac. de / Anefo for Nationaal Archief, CC0.
Source: en.wikipedia.org/wiki/Donovan#/media/File:Donovan_(1965).jpg (PD image).
Page 56 – Source: Montgomery Ward catalog, Summer 1966. (PD image).*

Page 57 – Models in office attire and tea dresses, early '50s. Creators unknown. Pre 1978, no copyright mark (PD image). – Jacqueline Kennedy on the steps of the Elysee Palace, France, 31st May 1961. From the JFK Library. Source: commons.wikimedia.org/wiki/File:President_De_Gaulle_stands_between_President_Kennedy_and_Mrs._Kennedy_on_the_steps_of_the_Elysee_Palace.jpg (PD image). – Jacqueline Kennedy in India, 1962. Source: flickr.com/photos/usembassy newdelhi/6914524677 by U.S. Embassy New Delhi. Attribution-NoDerivatives 4.0 International (CC BY-ND 4.0). – Jacqueline Kennedy at the White House 11th May 1962. Source: zh.m.wikipedia.org/wiki/File:JBKJFKMalraux.jpg. This photo is the property of the United States Government (PD image).
Page 58 – Mod fashions, source: vintag.es/2016/07/mod-fashion-characteristic-of-british.html. Pre 1978, (PD image).
Page 59 – Models wearing Mary Quant mini dresses, creator unknown. Source: thedabbler.co.uk/2012/10/granny-takes-a-trip-back-in-time/. Pre 1978, no copyright mark (PD image). – London street scene, creator unknown. Source: vintag.es/2016/07/mod-fashion -characteristic-of-british.html. Pre 1978, no copyright mark (PD image). – Mary Quant, 16th Dec 1966. Source: commons.wikimedia. org/wiki/File:Mary_Quant_in_a_minidress_(1966).jpg by Jac. de Nijs / Anefo from the Dutch National Archives. Licensed under the Creative Commons Attribution-Share Alike 3.0 Netherlands. – Models wearing Mary Quant plastic raincoats and boots, creator unknown. Pre 1978, no copyright mark (PD image).
Page 60 – From *Life* mag 7th Oct 1966. Source: books.google.com/books?id=jFYEAAAAMBAJ&printsec. (PD image).*
Page 61 – Penelope Tree, photographer Richard Avedon for Vogue Oct 1967. – Jean Shrimpton for Australian Vogue August 1965, Twiggy for Italian Vogue, July 1967, and various photo of Twiggy, dates, photographers, source unknown. Images reproduced this page under terms of Fair Use are used sparingly for information only, are significant to the article created and are rendered in low resolution to avoid piracy. It is believed that these images will not in any way limit the ability of the copyright owners to sell their product.
Page 62 – André Courrèges fur trimmed hat, creator unknown, source: alchetron.com/André-Courrèges. – Striped suits and slit glasses, creator unknown, source: vivavintageclothing.com/blog/a-salute-to-space-age-1960s-designer-andres-courreges/. – Cutout dress, photographed by William Laxton. Source: artlyst.com/news/andre-courreges-french-fashion-designer-painter-and-sculptor-dies-at-92/. – Space Bride by Jezebel, NY 1966. Images this page may be copyrighted by the creator. They are reproduced under fair use terms and rendered in low resolution to avoid piracy. It is believed these images will not in any way limit the ability of the copyright owner to market or sell their product.
Page 63 – Models wearing fashions from the late '60s. Photographers unknown. Pre 1978 (PD images). – The Beatles. Source: commons.wikimedia.org/wiki/File:The_Beatles_magical_mystery_tour_(cropped).jpg. Attrib 3.0 (CC BY 3.0).
Page 64 – From *Life* mag 4th Mar 1966. Source: books.google.com/books?id=LUwEAAAAMBAJ&printsec (PD image).*
Page 65 – Goodfellow in 1966, creator unknown. Source: engineeringhalloffame.org/profile-goodfellow.html. – HP 2116A, creator unknown. Source: computerhistory.org/timeline/computers/. Both images this page (PD image).
Page 66 – From *Life* mag 14th Oct 1966. Source: books.google.com/books?id=IFYEAAAAMBAJ&printsec. (PD image).*
Page 67 – From *Life* mag 7th Oct 1966. Source: books.google.com/books?id=jFYEAAAAMBAJ&printsec. (PD image).*
Page 68 – Adler win, creator unknown. Source: racingpast.ca/john_contents.php?id=171. Pre 1978, no mark (PD image). – Prince Philip, creator unknown. Source: insidethegames.biz/timelines/44. Pre 1978, no mark (PD image).
Page 69 – Ali, by Ira Rosenberg for World Journal Tribune, 1967. Source: commons.wikimedia.org/wiki/Category:Muhammad_Ali. (PD image). – Billie Jean King, creator unknown. (PD image). – Nicklaus, creator unknown. (PD image).
Page 70 – Gandhi in Washington, D.C. 1966, by Warren K. Leffler. Image from the Library of Congress. Digital ID: cph 3c34157. PD image. (PD image). – Mao ZeDong, source: commons.wikimedia.org/wiki/Category:Mao_Zedong_in_1966. (PD image). – Bhaktivedanta Swami in Golden Gate Park, 1967, by Mukunda Goswami. Source: commons.wikimedia.org/ wiki/Category:Hare_Krishna_movement_in_the_United_States. CC BY-SA 3.0 (PD image).
Page 71 – Reagan, source: en.wikipedia.org/wiki/1966_California_gubernatorial_election. CC BY-SA 4.0 (PD image). – 1966 New York City smog by Neal Boenzi for the NY Times. Image is for information only, as it is significant to the article and is reproduced under fair use terms. This image is rendered in low resolution to avoid piracy. It is believed this image will not in any way limit the ability of the copyright owner to sell their product.
Page 72-74 – All photos are, where possible, CC BY 2.0 or PD images made available by the creator for free use including commercial use. Where commercial use photos are unavailable, photos are included here for information only under U.S. fair use laws due to: 1- images are low resolution copies; 2- images do not devalue the ability of the copyright holders to profit from the original works in any way; 3- Images are too small to be used to make illegal copies for use in another book; 4- The images are relevant to the article created.
Page 75 – From *Life* mag 7th Oct 1966. Source: books.google.com/books?id=jFYEAAAAMBAJ&printsec. (PD image).*
Page 78 – From *Life* mag 18th Feb 1966. Source: books.google.com/books?id=IEwEAAAAMBAJ&printsec. (PD image).*
Page 79 – From *Life* mag 3rd Sept 1965. Source: books.google.com/books?id=nVIEAAAAMBAJ&printsec. (PD image).*

*Advertisement (or image from an advertisement) is in the public domain because it was published in a collective work (such as a periodical issue) in the US between 1925 and 1977 and without a copyright notice specific to the advertisement.
**Posters for movies or events are either in the public domain (published in the US between 1925 and 1977 and without a copyright notice specific to the artwork) or owned by the production company, creator, or distributor of the movie or event. Posters, where not in the public domain, and screen stills from movies or TV shows, are reproduced here under USA Fair Use laws due to: 1- images are low resolution copies; 2- images do not devalue the ability of the copyright holders to profit from the original works in any way; 3- Images are too small to be used to make illegal copies for use in another book; 4- The images are relevant to the article created.

This book was written by Bernard Bradforsand-Tyler as part of *A Time Traveler's Guide* series of books.

All rights reserved. The author exerts the moral right to be identified as the author of the work.

No parts of this book may be reproduced, stored in any retrieval system, or transmitted in any form or by any means, without prior written permission from the author.

This is a work of nonfiction. No names have been changed, no events have been fabricated. The content of this book is provided as a source of information for the reader, however it is not meant as a substitute for direct expert opinion. Although the author has made every effort to ensure that the information in this book is correct at time of printing, and while this publication is designed to provide accurate information in regard to the subject matters covered, the author assumes no responsibility for errors, inaccuracies, omissions, or any other inconsistencies herein and hereby disclaims any liability to any party for any loss, damage, or disruption caused by errors or omissions.

All images contained herein are reproduced with the following permissions:
- Images included in the public domain.
- Images obtained under creative commons license.
- Images included under fair use terms.
- Images reproduced with owner's permission.

All image attributions and source credits are provided at the back of the book. All images are the property of their respective owners and are protected under international copyright laws.

First printed in 2021 in the USA (ISBN 978-0-6450623-7-3).
Revised in 2024, 2nd Edition (ISBN 978-1-922676-34-4).
Self-published by B. Bradforsand-Tyler.

www.ingramcontent.com/pod-product-compliance
Lightning Source LLC
Chambersburg PA
CBHW072104110526
44590CB00018B/3314